Screwballs

Typeset and cover design by Bianca Ho
Illustrations by Agata Garbowska

Published by Golden Meteorite Press
126 Kingsway Garden
Post Office Box 34181
Edmonton, Alberta, Canada T5G 3G4
Telephone: 1-(780)-378-0063
Email: aamardon@yahoo.ca
Website: www.austinmardon.org

Library and Archives Canada Cataloguing in Publication
Mardon, Catherine A., 1962-, author
      Screwballs / Catherine Mardon.
ISBN 978-1-897472-54-5 (pbk.)
            1. Mardon, Catherine A., 1962-. 2. Lawyers--United States--
Biography. 3. Lawyers--Canada--Biography. I. Title.
KF373.M37A3 2014   340.092   C2014-904808-4

Dedicated to David and Arlene

Special thanks to Carmen Wu for her work and contribution

Screwballs

Catherine A. Mardon

Golden Meteorite Press

Table of Contents

Introduction 8

Whispering 9

Miss Somebody 15

David 19

Not a Practical Joke 24

Out of the Blue 30

Tony 34

Jean 40

Hidden Demons 45

And do Call me Shirley 52

Who am I 57

The Wild Man 64

The Gimp 69

The Black Hole 74

Arlene 81

Voices Again 92

Austin 96

Frat House Mom 102

Taking in Strays 107

Conclusion 120

INTRODUCTION

Anyone who knows me well, knows that I love baseball. Most of my life lessons come from on and off the field. My father had a heart attack when I was in grade school, and while he was recuperating, he taught me lots of different pitches. The one I could never master was the screwball, whether throwing it or trying to hit it. It does something completely unexpected. Throwing it requires you to move your arm in a weird and unnatural direction, and hitting it requires you to practically hit the ball backwards. It is basically the opposite of the more common curveball.

Very few pitchers have ever thrown the screwball; it's hard on your arm and even harder to master. Those big league pitchers who have mastered it can make batters look silly at the plate. They also tended to be some of the most memorable men to play the game. I asked my dad why they called it the screwball, and he told me you'd have to have a screw loose somewhere to want to learn it.

The word screwball has another meaning. It's usually used to describe people who don't act normally. Oddballs, weirdoes, and whatever other names used to describe people that aren't like everyone else. I've been called these names many times in my life, but I prefer to think of myself as simply eccentric. It can also be used as a pejorative for someone with a mental illness. There are probably more nicknames for the mentally ill than any other condition. I've known many in my life, and they have taught me many important life lessons. Although I have changed many of their names in order to preserve their privacy, this book is in their honor.

WHISPERING

Growing up in the South, people had a funny way of saying distressful things. I remember my grandmother telling us that someone had cancer, but the word cancer was always whispered. It was as if saying it out loud might bring the affliction down upon us. That was how mental illness was treated, if it was even mentioned at all.

My first introduction to the idea of people who had mental illnesses, was back in the day when gasoline prices were low enough to allow for Sunday drives. We decided to drive down to Norman and look at the campus of the University of Oklahoma. As we were driving around, we came upon buildings that had a collegial look to them, except that they had bars on the windows. My mom told us in a whisper that those buildings must be the state hospital.

In my young life, I had been to many hospitals. I was the youngest in my family on all sides, so I had visited many elderly relatives in hospitals and nursing homes. I also had adventurous older brothers who made regular trips to have things sewn back up or broken bones encased in plaster. I had never seen bars on hospital room windows before though. I was always full of questions, and my patient if not tired parents, had no answers to give me this time.

A few years passed before the topic came back up again, when one of our neighbors spent some time in the hospital with the barred windows. She had suffered from severe depression for many years. It was something everyone on the block knew, but we didn't speak about it. My mother's only response was that she couldn't imagine sitting around in a room with a bunch of strangers talking about her troubles.

Oklahoma is definitely one of those bastions of the Old West where everyone is expected to handle all their own problems without assistance. My mother had a very hard life. She endured severe illnesses, loss and hardships in her life that would have destroyed anyone without her inner strength. Still, there were times that she had trouble holding it together. She used to say that she had just "fallen apart" when she had one of those days. It was usually a day that was overcast or rainy.

I remember those rainy days as fun, because my mom would want me to play outside. I had permission to play in the street where the flash flooding rivers formed or splashing in big mud puddles. As long as I washed the mud off before coming inside, my mom didn't care. Other days, when she was feeling down in the dumps, her treatment of choice was cream filled pastry horns. I was her version of a drinking buddy at the bakery.

When my mom was mad, her treatment of choice was weeding the front yard. My father hated to mow the lawn. Mowing a lawn in Oklahoma when it was over 100 degrees outside wasn't anyone's idea of fun, really. My mother loved having a nice lawn, but my father refused to let her use fertilizer. As far as he was concerned, the faster the lawn died the better. When I came home to my mom on her knees weeding the front yard, I knew she was mad about something, usually my dad.

When she really felt bad, she'd go to the doctor for a hormone and vitamin shot. I had no idea what exactly that meant, but she always came home feeling better immediately. Still, the idea of seeking help for depression would never have crossed her mind. When she was in her 60's, she began seeing a doctor who only saw elderly women. I was a bit suspicious when I found out that this doctor was on probation from the medical association. I went with her to an appointment and found a waiting room full of little old ladies. I talked to the nurse at the desk, and she said the doctor couldn't even prescribe medications; all he did was make referrals.

She stayed in the examination room for over half an hour. So on the ride home, I asked her what the doctor did for her. She said he listened to her. Basically all these women went to a disbarred doctor who couldn't actually do anything for them except listen to them, rather than go to a psychologist or psychiatrist, because going to a shrink would have been societal suicide. My mom would never have wanted people whispering about her.

My dad was whispered about though. He'd had an even harder life than my mom. He lost most of his family in the Spanish Flu epidemic in 1918. He was only 3 years old when he was orphaned. He was raised by his widowed grandmother in a New York City tenement building. He had to quit school and go to work during the Depression when his grandmother became too ill to continue taking in laundry to support them. When his grandmother died, he entered the army before World War II started.

During the war, my father saw many things that wounded his soul. He rarely spoke about it, but he couldn't hide it. He had spent time after the war in a VA Hospital. He had horrific nightmares. Alcohol seemed to be the only thing that gave him any relief. Today he would be diagnosed with PTSD, but to his generation, silence and sucking it up were expected. I often wonder how much he might have accomplished in his life had he had access to current PTSD treatment.

I have four half-brothers in addition to my one full brother. Growing up though, I didn't know the difference. I thought it was normal for brothers and sisters to have different last names. I think I was a teenager before I actually understood that my older brothers had a different father. My parents had gotten together when my brothers were pre-schoolers. Their father had also suffered from PTSD from his service in World War II. My mother described him to me as a gentle, quiet man, a very skilled mechanic. During the war he had served in the same unit as Audie Murphy. He saw an incredible amount of front line action, and after the war he wasn't the same. He would go out for a loaf of bread and not come home for two weeks. He took on a Jekyll and Hyde personality, and they separated every time the Mr. Hyde came out, and got back together during those times when he was more stable.

He gambled. Sometimes to pay a gambling debt, he would put my grandfather down as guarantor on his checks. When they bounced, my grandparents would be called, and they would make good on the worthless checks in order to preserve their standing in the community. It humiliated my mother. When she became pregnant in 1947, he joined the Air Force in order to have insurance coverage for my mother. She only had one kidney, having lost one at the age of 17. Her father thought she got pregnant because she wanted to die; she had been advised not to have children due to the stress it might place upon her remaining kidney. He was allowed to re-enter at his former master sergeant rank. The order the military gave him seemed to give him some stability. Three years later he found himself in Korea, and being back in a war again, caused a complete psychotic break.

They found him wandering the streets in Tokyo, unable to remember his name or how he had gotten from Korea to Japan. He was arrested for desertion and court martialed, and ultimately was busted down to a private. By this time my mother had a toddler and an infant, and couldn't make ends meet on a private's salary. She contacted the Red Cross to help her get him home on a hardship discharge. From there, he went straight into the hospital, and my mom got three jobs to support the family. An elderly neighbor provided free child care, but my mom lived in fear that social services were going to take her children away. At the VA hospital, he was diagnosed with schizophrenia. His behavior became completely unpredictable. This was decades before there was any real treatment for this illness. He pushed my mother out of a moving car when she was pregnant, and she lost the child. She knew then that she would have to permanently separate from him.

He spent the next 15 years in and out of mental hospitals. She rarely knew where he was. He began writing hot checks again, which came back to her. She worked mornings at a downtown diner, days at a BBQ restaurant, and evenings at a parking lot toll booth. His creditors started coming after her, and so to protect herself, she knew she had to divorce him. The problem was, she didn't have money for an attorney, and didn't know where her husband was to serve him with the papers. The owner of the Hickory Inn restaurant she worked at offered to pay for the attorney and newspaper notices required, since no one knew where he was. She was apprehensive about becoming indebted to him, but had no choice. The day her divorce was granted, her boss asked her to come into his office. She said she figured that he was going to expect "payment". Instead, he just wanted to see if she was okay. He moved her from waitress to the catering staff, which gave her a raise large enough to allow her to stop her parking lot job. She told me that he was one of the nicest men she ever knew. When he died the summer before I left for college, we went to his funeral. It's one of the few times I ever saw my mother cry.

She rarely heard from her ex-husband again. She would sometimes hear stories about him when she took my brothers to visit their dad's family. He was in and out of the VA hospital. He eventually committed suicide when he could no longer endure his illness. He was released from the VA in Kansas City, checked into a hotel, and jumped out of the 6th floor window. Even today, with state of the art treatments, 10% of those diagnosed with schizophrenia are dead within 10 years of diagnosis, most by suicide. At least 40% attempt suicide. Back before treatments, the suicide rate was even higher. His sons didn't remember him; the only father they ever knew was our dad.

Although I didn't understand the difficulties my parents went through, as a child I instinctively knew that when my parents didn't feel well, it wasn't them. It was something separate from them. So when my mom had the blues, I didn't get mad at her, I got mad at IT. When I was woken up at night by my father's screams, I was never mad at him, I was mad at the nightmares. I wasn't sure what IT was, but I knew IT made my parents different. That ability to separate someone from their mental illness became important for me as I went through life. My mother always told me that everything happens for a reason. My father told me that God only gives you what you can handle; that life's difficulties are God's way of strengthening our muscles to carry our crosses.

They were both right. My childhood had well prepared me for the life that God had chosen for me.

MISS SOMEBODY

I think my first real encounter with someone with a mental illness happened in 6th grade. Going to a parochial school, I had small classes, and by that time we all knew each other really well. I loved school. I even loved taking tests. I was however, one of those students that really needed to be kept busy. If my math classes hadn't been at my own pace, I would have spent a lot of time in the principal's office. After math, I loved science.

That year we got a new science teacher, so we were all excited. Well, maybe just me, but any change was good. At first she seemed okay, but after about a month she seemed to have lost her way. Several times a week she had us copy things out of science dictionaries for the entire class. It didn't bother me much at first, because reading encyclopaedias had been a favorite past time of mine. Still, I could tell there was something weird going on.

A group of 20 kids sitting around and copying stuff out of dictionaries is going to eventually blow up. We all tried to find things to do to keep ourselves from going a bit nuts. Lisa began doing her nails, Mark started cleaning the cafeteria style table top with his eraser, and I worked on homework from other classes. I saw many heads nod and jerk as people fell asleep. When I told my parents about it, my mom found it hard to believe, and my father complained that he wasn't paying tuition for me to just sit in study hall.

Most of the time our teacher had her head down reading something. I'm not sure how it started, but we began this game where one of us would make a quiet strange noise, and then slowly ramp up the volume until our teacher looked up, and then got silent. After she went back to reading, someone on the other side of the room would do the same thing. When she looked up the other direction, silence again. Eventually she asked us if anyone had heard a strange noise. We all swore that we couldn't hear anything.

This game of trying to freak out the teacher, or maybe just get her attention, went on for weeks. She began to look frazzled. She started missing class at least once a week. That was no better, because our class would be taken over by the principal, a very stern Carmelite nun. During one of those absences, our principal noticed the half cleaned table that Mark had produced. He was threatened with exorcism or amputation, I can't remember which. After a few days, the teacher would come back looking better, but as soon as she made us start copying out of books again, the noises returned.

Eventually, she stopped coming entirely. One day we came to class, and our pastor was in the room in addition to the principal. We were told that our science teacher wouldn't be returning. She had experienced a mental breakdown and was in the hospital. I was pretty sure they meant the one with the bars on the windows. Most of my classmates didn't seem bothered, except that our math teacher was now going to teach our science classes too. I felt guilty. I still do, I suppose. Years later, I heard the whole story.

This teacher had been teaching in a public middle school, where she had an affair with the married principal. When she became pregnant, he started pressuring her to have an abortion. Eventually she agreed. It went badly, and she was told that she would never be able to have children again. After this, the principal dumped her and started an affair with the band teacher. She wanted him back, and made the mistake of threatening to expose him to his wife.

The principal used his authority to get her evaluations downgraded. First she was placed on probation, then suspension, and eventually was terminated. That wasn't enough though; he made sure that she lost her license to teach as well. She came to teach at our school, because back then parochial schools didn't require teaching certificates. She had begun to believe the evaluations that her ex-boyfriend had labeled her with; she had lost her spark, and her confidence. She was fragile, depressed, and not ready for the pranks that Catholic school kids were famous for.

After she got out of the hospital, she went to work as an educational book salesman. She did that for a few years, making more money than she would have as a teacher. She re-built her life, but she still missed the classroom. One day she was sitting in a school office waiting for an appointment with an assistant principal that she hoped to get a big order from, when she spotted a notice on the bulletin board. It advertised jobs in foreign countries for teachers. She wrote the number down and kept it in her purse for weeks before getting up the nerve to call.

She thought about it, talked to family and friends about it, and eventually she found herself teaching English in a school in Korea. A few years there, and she went on to a school in Venezuela, then Switzerland, and eventually the Middle East. When I saw her again after 25 years, she looked older, but fit and happy. She assured me that our gaslight treatment hadn't been the cause of her breakdown. She was headed there before she met our class.

She had been one of those people who had built their whole world around their career. All she ever wanted to be was a teacher, and her self-esteem and her world view had been based around being a teacher. She likened it to someone who plays pro football. They have spent their whole life dreaming to be a ball player, preparing for it, and then age or injury ends that. If you haven't built a life outside of football, you don't know what to do. She had assumed that she would teach in that same school until she was too old to get out of bed. It was all she was, and all she wanted to be.

Losing her job was bad, but being labeled as a bad teacher was worse. It was as if by killing her vision of herself that he had killed her soul. She went back to teaching because she loved it, but she had added lots of other stuff to her life so that teaching was no longer her whole sense of self. She had become a country collector. I thought she meant having a country theme to her home decorating. Instead, she literally meant that she collected country stamps in her passport.

With every day off or weekend, she traveled. While she was in Korea, she went to almost every Asian country. While in Switzerland, she bought a Euro rail pass and slept on the train and went sightseeing in a different country every day. She was looking forward to exploring Africa next. She still loved to teach, but it wasn't her whole world now, the world was. She showed me pictures of temples and cathedrals, and lots and lots of children. Most of the time she taught the children of American and British diplomats or businessmen. At night, she taught kids whose parents couldn't afford to send them to such expensive schools.

She made herself whole again. I thought about her later when I had to face up to career-ending injuries. I had fallen into the same trap, placing much of my self-worth into a title, a job description. We are all going to end up with holes along the way. We can fill them, or we can keep falling in them.

DAVID

I became an aunt at the tender age of 7. I became a babysitter at an age when most children still need a babysitter. When I was 10 and my nephew, David, was 3 and his younger brother was only 6 months old, my brother, their father, fractured his neck. He had been in a bad car accident, and he and his wife had recently broken up. They had married really young, and she had developed a bad case of post-partum depression. His wife had a family history of depression, and she had endured the trauma as a child of discovering her father after he had committed suicide.

At the custody hearing, they both told the judge that they weren't up to having custody. Each tried to force custody on the other. They were so young that they didn't understand what not taking custody would mean. The judge didn't want to place the boys in foster care. He looked around the room, and saw my mother. She was in court that day because my brother couldn't drive himself yet. The judge looked at her and she said she knew from his eyes what he was going to ask. He asked her to take custody of the boys. She told me later that she felt like history was re-peating itself. She had fought to keep her boys out of foster care, and now she would do the same for her grandsons.

Today grandparents routinely get custody of their grandchildren. In the early 70's, it wasn't as common. Our very small house quickly became bursting at the seams. My younger nephew was sickly and had to have a special, and therefore expensive, formula. As a baby he naturally got the lion's share of our attention, and David began to act out. His mom's illness, his father's injury, his parent's divorce, all disrupted his life. He became almost unmanageable, and everything that my mother tried with him failed. The financial strain and the emotional stress of taking care of both boys caused fights between my parents that I had never seen before.

Years later, my father told me that coming home every night reminded him of his childhood. His father had died when he was 6 months old, and so his mother moved back to live with her own widowed mother. His brothers were 3 and 5 years old at the time. When he was 3 years old, his mother died too. When he was 5, his middle brother was killed in the street by an ice wagon. After that, his oldest brother who was just 10 years old, began acting out. His grandmother couldn't cope, and she sent my uncle to live with his other grandfather. Taking my nephews in had brought up the memories of all his childhood pain, as if he was watching a rerun in his head. Eventually, one of the boys needed to go. My mother kept the baby, and David went back to live with his father.

This began a ping pong life for David. He had learned at an early age that if he wasn't happy, he could act out and get what he wanted, or get moved. He went back and forth between his mother and father, who alternately tried to buy his affection or tried to use tough love. By the age of 14, he was an alcoholic. My brother had recently remarried a woman who had two small daughters. David began to act out in a way that made them worry that he was going to do something inappropriate with his new step sisters. He couldn't be sent back to his mother this time, because she had been hospitalized for depression. My mother called and asked me if I could take him in.

At the time I became his guardian, I was a 22 year old law student. When I should have been studying property law, I was having meetings with his principal about his truancy. I had no idea how to force a teenager to attend school. I had always loved school and couldn't imagine anyone not wanting to go. He drained my liquor cabinet; I so rarely drank that I didn't notice at first. When caught, he told people that I had bought the liquor for him. He went joy-riding in my car when I was asleep. I didn't discover that until the police came to my door. It's a wonder that I didn't flunk out of school. Instead of being a parent to him, I tried to be his friend. I treated him like a roommate, and it failed miserably. I was barely older than a teenager myself, and didn't know how to take care of another person, let alone someone so rebellious.

At the end of the year, my mother saw how drained it had made me and how badly I had done in school that semester, and made my brother take him back. David was shortly returned to his mother, and then began several years of rehab attempts. By the time I was asked to take him in again, he was 19 years old, and straight from detox. He did practically every drug that was available at the time. I was a busy attorney and didn't have much to give him except a warm bed. I got him a job that he would never go to, and instead he mostly sat at home watching MTV. I never knew what I would find when coming home from work.

On an ordinary day off, I went to my tool shed to get my drill to do some minor maintenance job around the house, only to discover that all my power tools had been pawned. I was absolutely livid. Since I was housing and feeding him, I knew that my tools had been used for drug money. As it was a holiday weekend, I had to wait several days to find out if my tools were still available to be redeemed or if they had been lost per-manently. After I got them back, I gave him an ultimatum. He had to go to work, or get out. He went for about two weeks, long enough for a pay check, and then he went partying with friends and got into a car with a drunk driver who had a wreck that injured David's back just enough to prevent him from going back to his grocery stocking job.

I had had enough. By the time he had recuperated, he received a cash settlement from the insurance company for the wreck. I told him that he now had enough money to find another place to live. Instead of looking for an apartment, he went to a pool hall in the worst part of Oklahoma City. My nephew was 5'6", of slight build, blond haired and blue eyed. He always looked much younger than his actual age and still didn't need to shave. How he thought he could hold his own in a lion's den, I'll never know. He was robbed of all his money, and showed up back on my door step in fright-soiled blue jeans. I put him in my car, and dropped him off at a friend's house. During the ride he kept saying that he couldn't believe I was throwing him away.

I occasionally got messages on my phone for money or disconnected gibberish that I couldn't understand. One evening, he and a friend were so drunk and high that they broke into a vacant apartment to sleep it off, and woke up in jail. There was a desperate call from the county jail, asking for me to please come bail him out. I refused. I told myself at the time that I had to protect myself, and I couldn't guarantee that he would actually show up for court, and didn't want my reputation affected. Deep down though, I just knew that he had to begin to experience real consequences for his actions, or he would never change.

When they finally released him after a couple of months, he didn't call me to come get him. Instead, I found my home burglarized and vandalized. I had no doubt that he was behind it, but he was nowhere to be found. The next time I got a call from jail, I refused to accept the charges. I knew that he had been making the rounds of all my brothers, his mother's brother, and both sets of grandparents, but he always overstayed his welcome. My mother also refused his calls from jail this time. She said it was one of the hardest things she had ever done. The last time I saw him was a year later. He showed up at my door and said he was homeless. I told him that I had a roommate, so there was nowhere for him sleep. Then he wanted to borrow my tent, to which I refused, and gave him the name of a friend who worked at a homeless shelter. He refused that offer, and walked away.

A few years later I got a call that he had been murdered. He had been working the streets of Tulsa as a prostitute, and he had been stabbed to death by a John in a fight about money or drugs. It didn't matter, the Tulsa police refused to arrest David's killer. As far as they were concerned, no human was involved. It took them two weeks to bother informing his parents that he was dead. My mother told me that she had talked to him about 6 months before, and he told her that his girlfriend had had a baby. We never found out if that was the truth, or where the child might be.

What David taught me is that some people die before they have a chance to hit their rock bottom and truly seek help. All of us would have been willing to help him get real help, but we weren't willing to help him continue to live a life that was destroying him. He obviously needed not only drug and alcohol rehabilitation, but also psychiatric intervention. His mother had a history of depression. His grandfather had Schizophrenia. In fact, both his grandfathers had committed suicide. He had the genetic predispositions for both substance abuse and mental illness. However, a person truly has to want to change and be willing to seek help for any kind of treatment to work.

There just isn't a way to properly explain the despair that can come from watching someone you love self-destruct, and be completely powerless to help. I refuse to give money to panhandlers. It may seem odd considering how much of my time I've invested into helping the homeless, but I know that giving someone money on the street is enabling them to stay on the street for another day rather than getting help. When we keep them from hitting bottom hard enough to rebound, we are helping them slowly slide down into a pit. They don't need money. They need help, and won't get it on the street.

NOT A PRACTICAL JOKE

When I thought about attending law school, it was not with the idea that I was going to become rich. I graduated from college with a degree that was not going to allow me to attend either graduate school or obtain a job. By the time I discovered this, it was too late for me to pick a different major without repeating most of my undergraduate work. I'd hate to say that I went to law school simply because I got in, but I applied after taking some business law classes that I did really well in. My professor asked me to take the entrance exam, and I did really well on it. I had truthfully never considered law school, but once I did, I thought about how interesting it might be.

I did love the idea of working with the poor or disadvantaged. Right out of school I was hired to work for an ecumenical organization that had a variety of ministries. My primary work was in helping family farmers keep their farms. I also got to help out on a variety of other ministries, such as with refugees or disaster relief. This put me into contact with other non-profits. I got to volunteer with cases through legal aid, a variety of social justice organizations, and the local homeless shelter. After a lifetime of always being the youngest, always sitting at the kid's table, I finally felt like a grown up.

My work at the homeless shelter was very rewarding. During this hard economic time, there were lots of people in the homeless shelter or living in their cars nearby, who had never been homeless before. A job loss, a family illness or disability, could very quickly put a family out on the street. For those who simply needed a job, I wasn't much help. I got called in when someone needed help applying for disability. In the beginning this was usually someone who had been injured off the job and could no longer work in their old professions. There are lots of attorneys to help people injured on the job.

I dealt with a self-employed long haul truck driver who had broken both legs and had his truck repossessed when he couldn't work. I helped part-time workers who didn't have insurance when they became sick or had to have surgery. The largest group I worked with were those who had been diagnosed with AIDS. During the early years of the epidemic, when someone found out they were sick, they often lost their jobs, their home, and their friends and family. Helping them obtain disability benefits not only got them out of the homeless shelter where their compromised immune systems were under constant attack, it allowed them to obtain medication.

In the beginning there wasn't any real treatment for AIDS, except to try to prolong their lives until a time when there might be a breakthrough in treatment. Back before there was a blood test to diagnosis AIDS, you qualified for disability based on whether certain opportunistic infections were present. Men were the largest original group with the infection, and so when the disability regulations were first drawn up, only the infections that men suffered from were listed. As more women began to come down with the illness, it became apparent that females suffered from different opportunistic infections. Women didn't come down with Kaposi's sarcoma, but instead developed things like fungal infections of the mouth, throat, or vagina. This proved to be quite a fight, but in the end bureaucrats were forced to recognize the infections women suffered from, so that they could begin receiving benefits as well.

The downside of being one of the few attorneys in Oklahoma who would take on clients with AIDS was that I ended up going to a lot of funerals for young men. Way too many funerals. I had watched many older family members slowly go downhill as they aged. They would go to funeral homes and slowly slip away, usually after long lives, and many children and grandchildren. These kids that were dying were different. They were my age or even younger. They had their whole lives ahead of them. Yet, they wasted away just as fast as my 80–90 year old relatives. When it got around in the local bar association that I was helping people with AIDS, some ostracized me. I had people I had gone to law school with, get up and move to the other side of the room and away from me at bar association functions.

I was given a gift by these clients. They showed me how you can be thrown away by society, but still maintain your dignity. I had people tell me that the illness was a punishment from God. That wasn't the God I knew. Understanding his will is way above my pay grade, but an illness isn't a punishment. It is a vile thing, but hearing people discuss innocent victims versus those who deserved the illness, made me sick. My work in this community taught me many things about stigma that would help me later in my life among the mentally ill.

Helping the disabled get their benefits helped ease the overcrowding in the shelter. When the economy began to improve, we were able to thin out the employable, and then we were left with the traditionally hard to house: the alcoholics, the addicts and the mentally ill. Being naïve, I assumed those three labels were separate. I soon found out that it was difficult to put definitive labels on people. Some of my people had started with street drugs, but a life on the streets had left them with mental illnesses from the traumas they had endured. Some had turned to street drugs to self-medicate mental illnesses. It was very difficult to decide which came first. I eventually realized that it didn't matter; both had to be dealt with for anyone to successfully transition from a life on the streets.

My first mentally ill client was Gregg. He didn't live in the homeless shelter, but often came there to eat. I was asked by one of the social workers to go to his grandmother's house and help fill out disability paperwork for him. It's not unusual for the mentally ill to live with relatives. His grandmother was right out of a Hollywood movie; she looked exactly like a grandmother should, right down the house dress covered by a lacy apron. She led me through her kitchen to the garage door. When she opened it, she said, "Gregg, there is someone here to see you." Then she stepped back to allow me through the door.

I thought I had stepped into a nuclear reactor. Every surface, every wall and door had been covered in aluminum foil. There were coat hangers suspended from the ceiling with long strips of foil trailing from them. It was like some 1950's low budget science fiction movie set. I took a deep breath. I had been known to pull practical jokes on people. My first reaction was that someone was playing a joke on me. Yet, when I looked at Gregg sitting in the middle of the garage on an old army cot, there was something in his eyes that told me this was no joke. I decided to right then to ignore everything I saw, and focus on my client.

As it turned out, Gregg was intelligent, gentle, and scared of his own shadow. He taught me a lot of things about schizophrenia. He had a great deal of difficulty understanding body language. I normally speak very animatedly with my hands, but had to be careful with him. If I waved my hands around in certain way, he became afraid that I was trying to read his thoughts. Because he could not read body language, he didn't understand how anyone else could, so when I could guess how he was feeling based on his body language, he assumed I must be reading his mind. He also did not understand hints or hidden agenda. I could not beat around the bush with him. I had to be quite blunt. That was difficult for me to cope with. I had been raised to treat people with gentleness. I had to learn that true gentleness comes from treating people where they are, and making them feel at ease, even if that meant, in Gregg's case, to treat him with straight-faced abruptness.

Gregg had been properly medicated for several years until he turned 18, and his parent's insurance company quit covering his medications. His parents couldn't afford his medications, which cost several hundred dollars a month. They tried for several months to find a way to pay for them, but in the end, they said they had three other children at home to be concerned with too. They also knew that as long as they continued to attempt to care for him, the government wouldn't step in to help. So they had to let him go. Without his medication, he wandered the streets talking to himself. His parents often followed him at night to make sure he was okay.

His grandmother collaborated with her physician to have him prescribe for her the medicine that Gregg needed. He couldn't prescribe them all, or in the same dosages, but it was enough to stabilize Gregg somewhat. He moved into her garage and his family attempted to get him signed up for permanent disability benefits. He was turned down. There are no blood tests or brain scans to definitively diagnose mental illnesses. I took on his appeal and fought for him as if he was sitting on death row. Considering the suicide rates of the mentally ill, perhaps he was.

I found my way to the Murrah Building in Oklahoma City, and on the first floor was the Social Security Administration. It seemed like I spent every lunch hour there for seven years filing disability applications. Gregg was my first client with schizophrenia, but not my last. It may seem silly to turn someone with schizophrenia down for disability. It's actually quite common for everyone to be turned down initially. The government believes that if you really can work, you will go to work rather than appealing their decision. If you truly can't work, then you will still be out of work when your appeal goes forward. The fact that disabled people are having to live without financial support or medical benefits for up to two years does not terribly concern the powers that be.

After Gregg began to receive benefits, he settled into a small apartment. Stable on his medication, his apartment was full of books, not aluminum foil. In the 90's when new medications came on the market, he began to do so well that he went back to school part time. The last I heard from him, he was close to receiving a degree in English Literature. He will likely never be hired to teach, or be admitted to a graduate program. What high school or college would hire a teacher with an illness that scares everyone? To Gregg though, his receiving a diploma seemed like a justification for his life. Those with mental illnesses often struggle with "why me?"

Stigma is obviously difficult to live with. It's hard for those with schizo-phrenia to find and hold a job, make and keep friends, or even go on a date. No mother wants to brag that her son has schizophrenia, and that he's currently homeless and living in the alley behind a massage parlor downtown. They expect to receive stigma from society, but sometimes the hardest stigma comes from friends and family, and even from themselves. With a serious mental illness, a person feels worthless or defective. I've often thought it would be much easier to accept a mental illness if there was a blood test for it. Seeing a lab report or an x-ray must make it easier to accept having a physical illness.

Instead, it can take months or years to get an accurate diagnosis and proper medication. In that time a lot of damage can be done to a person's rela-tionships with their friends and family. It can be very difficult to convince a person to stay on their medication; taking the medication is the accepting the label. When psychotic, a person might be a knight in King Author's court or a werewolf. When on their medication, they are someone that peo-ple treat like dirt. They live in the poorest part of town on government assistance, or even spend their lives on the street eating from dumpsters. Given that as a choice, most of us would choose the Round Table.

The most important thing a person with a mental illness needs is a reason to stay on their medication, and a reason to get out of bed in the morning. They need things in their life to give them purpose and meaning. Some-times that can be part time job or a volunteer position. Sometimes it might just be a pet that depends on them, or a circle of friends with the same illness, something that gives them life, and a reason to live. There have been people in history who think that those with serious mental ill-nesses are better off dead than suffering. I believe that we are all given crosses, and those with mental illnesses are given very heavy crosses, but that doesn't mean their lives aren't worth living. Life is the greatest gift we are given. So long as there is life, there is hope. Every life is worth-while, and of equal dignity.

OUT OF THE BLUE

I never knew what I was going to be asked to do or who I would meet when I got a call from the homeless shelter to come to visit. When I walked into the small office I used to deal with people in some semblance of confidentiality, I was introduced to a man who looked like a typical Okie. He was wearing boots and jeans, and had the skin and hands that told me he was used to hard work outside. He was a quiet man, and at first I assumed that he was one of the many men I dealt with who had been injured, on the job or off, and could no longer do the only job they had ever known how to do, and ended up in the homeless shelter. I was wrong.

His name was Sam. I was right that he'd been a hard worker in his life. He had started working on oil rigs when he was 16, and he did all the things you were supposed to do as a man in Oklahoma. He'd married, had children, bought a house and truck, and took off every fall when hunting season started. He'd had a few injuries along the way, broken hand, nasty cut on his leg, but a couple of years ago, he had something big hit him on the head. His hard hat had saved his life, but he'd still been knocked unconscious for several hours and spent several days in the hospital.

While at home recuperating, he began to feel weird, as if he didn't really belong in his own body. He started watching shows on television he normally wouldn't have. He caught himself thinking about what it would feel like to wear his wife's clothing. One day while she was at work, he began trying them on. He got so involved in it, that he lost track of time, and his wife came home to finding almost all her clothes on the bed. He convinced her that he had gotten bored, and decided to reorganize her closet. She seemed suspicious, but mollified.

As the weeks went on, he couldn't escape the overwhelming feeling that he was a woman in a man's body. By this time, I had met many people with gender issues, and somehow he just didn't seem to fit. As I took a closer look at him, I did notice that his face seemed hairless. One thing about working around the homeless, is that the men are rarely perfectly clean shaven. The rules in most shelters are that everyone has to leave early in the morning, so those who shave and shower usually do so at night. In Sam's case, he told me that he had spent several thousand dollars on electrolysis. Not only was his face hairless, but so was several other parts of his body.

He had eventually told his wife that he was thinking about undergoing a sexual reassignment surgery. She promptly filed for divorce and got full custody of their children. He moved into an apartment and went back to work. In his evenings, he began to hang out in gay bars with other transsexuals. He found a therapist who helped people who were considering surgery. He began to have problems at work. Apparently someone had seen him entering the gay bar, and with his recent divorce, the rumor began to circulate that he was gay.

Oil rigs then were very macho zones. The few women who worked there often had to become "one of the boys" in appearance and personality in order to survive the harsh work environment. He started to experience teasing, then taunting, and then outright harassment. He endured it primarily for his kids. He wanted to make sure he could pay his child support. Eventually, he began going through the steps necessary before he would be approved for surgery. In addition to electrolysis and therapy, he would be required to live an entire year as a woman before being allowed to have the surgery. The first day he appeared at work wearing Gloria Vanderbilt jeans and a pink blouse with a matching hard hat, he was fired.

He had contested his firing at the union and to the state's employment authorities, to no avail. He began to go through his savings, so he moved in with a friend, and began tending at a bar at a local gay club. He cashed in his retirement to continue paying the same level of child support, even though his income was a quarter what it had been. He told me he didn't want his kids and ex-wife to be punished because of his new circumstances. I also think in the beginning he truly thought he would be allowed to go back to work once his employment appeal was heard.

Sexual re-assignment surgery is quite expensive. At the time, no insurance covered even a portion of the costs. Male to female is significantly cheaper than the other direction, but it was still very costly. Doctors and hospitals usually want payment in full before the procedure. Electrolysis of the face and body may well be cosmetic, but there are areas that need to be hair-free for the surgery itself. Sometimes in my work I heard or saw things that I had never imagined. When he began to explain, I put my hand up to stop him, saying that I really didn't need to know all the details.

In the last months counting down to his surgery date, he said he began to experience some strange things. He had been uncomfortable when a nice looking man commented on his appearance after the hormonal therapy caused him to grow large breasts. This really puzzled me because the man who sat in the chair in front of me had no discernable bust line. He also caught himself checking out cute girls that walked by him, which he hadn't done in almost two years. He brought these things up to his therapist, and she told him that it was common to have some second thoughts when approaching the surgery, and it was why they required people to live as the other gender for a year before surgery.

He tried to put his fears to rest. The night before his surgery, he couldn't sleep. He felt all different again, like he had right after his head injury. When the surgeon came in to talk to him, they both decided that it was best to postpone the surgery for the time being. The surgeon sent him back to his psychiatrist, who in turn sent him to a neurologist. The neurologist told him that serious head injuries can lead to major personality changes. Sometimes these changes are temporary, and sometimes permanent. It was ultimately decided that his gender issues were a result of the head injury, and his brain had begun the healing process.

He had lost his career, his family, his retirement, and all his friends. What money he had invested in the surgery was gone. The money he had left went to the mastectomy that made him begin to feel like a man again. He was nearly penniless, homeless, and unemployed. He had a warrant out for his arrest for being delinquent on his child support. I had my work cut out for me.

It never ceased to amaze me how a disability can completely destroy a person's life. I eventually got him on disability. He wasn't going to be on it permanently, but he needed some time to get back on his feet. His head injury had been at the heart of all his problems. He finally had the opportunity to reconcile with his children. His ex-wife had remarried, but I believe hearing the explanation of what had happened to her former husband gave her some relief. She had been blaming herself for not being enough of a woman or for not knowing that there was something wrong with her husband.

He eventually re-trained as a long haul truck driver. That allowed him to have a place to sleep, and have long periods of time where he could think deep thoughts. He said that he had never put any real thought into his life before his accident. He didn't know if it was the head injury, or all that he'd been through since it, but he felt like he was actually working his brain in a way he had never before.

I think the main thing I learned from Sam is that no matter how far we have fallen, and no matter how bad things seem, we can always start again. When the landing craft heading to Utah Beach during the Normandy invasion put the troops well out of position from where they were supposed to land, the Commander, General Theodore Roosevelt Jr., said, "We'll start the war from here!" That's how Sam decided to live the rest of his life. He wasn't were he planned to be, or even wanted to be, but he decided to just start from where he found himself, and get on with the business of living.

TONY

Of all the AIDS patients I had as clients, Tony stands out in my mind the clearest. I picture him sitting in his living room on a stack of moving boxes, but that's not how we began. I first met him at a food bank run just for people with AIDS; they weren't really welcome at the regular food bank. Back then when people saw someone who was emaciated and had Kaposi's marks on their face, they freaked out. Lots of people thought AIDS was contagious like the flu, that you could get it from a toilet seat or from a public swimming pool. It may seem silly now, but at the time, people had more fear than education.

This food bank was a little different anyway. Most food banks give canned and boxed food, plus day old bread donated from grocery stores. This one gave out microwaveable meals. Most were made by local churches in large bunches and then portioned out. People with AIDS didn't often have the energy to cook anything, and they routinely fought with nausea. Simple meals that were high in calories and were easy to digest were what this food bank gave out, in addition to cases of meal replacement drinks and some fresh fruit.

I had been asked to meet Tony by a friend of mine from church. She took people with AIDS to their doctor's appointments. Many were just too frail to drive even if they had money for a car. He looked like he weighed 50 pounds. I was afraid someone was going to bump into him and knock him across the room. He was stooped over and walked with a cane, but looked vaguely familiar. I normally have a good memory for faces, even if people's names often escaped me.

We started talking and I realized where I knew him from. We had once played opposite each other in a church softball league. He had been an architect. He had done really well, working his way up in a large firm, when he decided to open his own office. He made a great deal of money very quickly. Leaving the large firm resulted in him losing his health insurance. He was young and healthy at the time and thought he had lots of time to worry about getting private coverage. It was a gamble he lost. He ended up in the hospital with pneumonia just months after making the move.

Unable to find the energy to work, he had no real income. He had bought a large home not far from the state capital. It was an area of oil baron era mansions, and many had long ago been broken up into apartments. Some blocks had become little more than a row of crack houses. Slowly though, people who wanted to live closer to downtown, or those who loved the older architectural features, began to reclaim these precious old ladies. Tony had put thousands of dollars and months of effort into his home. It was his passion, and eventually it became his Ark.

In Oklahoma, creditors can't touch your home. It's a remnant of home-steading past, and a reflection of how many busts our economy has experienced. Our creditor laws are designed to allow a person to get back up on their feet without losing everything. Tony started renting out the ample rooms in his home to others who had been evicted after becoming ill. Not having an income or insurance, his only option for health care was the medical students you could see for free at the university hospital.

He wanted to get on disability so that he could afford to go to Mexico to try an experimental treatment. I had heard about these miracle cures; I had even had a client die on a bus trying to make the trip. In my opinion, they were just another snake oil scam marketed to a desperate population. I knew though, that hope can keep a person alive longer. At that time, everyone was trying to stay alive as long as possible in the belief that a cure or treatment might come at any time.

His disability forms were very straight forward, and he was approved relatively quickly. It didn't help his health insurance issues though. When someone goes on Social Security in the US due to reaching retirement age, their Medicare benefits start immediately. When you are approved for Social Security Disability, your insurance doesn't start for two years. Usually a person can fill those two years with coverage by low income Medicaid. Tony didn't qualify for Medicaid due to the value of his home.

Ironically, having to depend on free health care at the university saved his life. He was asked to join in a research project for an experimental treatment. He was told realistically it might buy him an extra year, and some extra energy to be able to enjoy that extra year. About a month after starting the treatment, he said he really did feel better. He had accepted that it wasn't going to last, and wanted to do the things that people with limited time do. He wanted to take a trip of a lifetime, and he had always thought about backpacking across Europe. He knew he couldn't do that, so he decided to take an extended cruise.

He cashed out his life insurance. Many companies will allow you to access your life insurance for 50% of face value if you can get a doctor to sign the forms that you will die within the next two years. Their primary focus had been on cancer patients until the AIDS epidemic hit. He thought that with a cruise, there would be a doctor on board, and he could fly home from any port of call. His biggest obstacle was in getting his medication while at sea. Researchers usually want to see people in their offices in order to chart their progress for research parameters.

In the case of some of these early retro-virus studies, their only real parameter was simply how long someone lived on the drug. They had gotten permission to experiment with AIDS drugs well before they normally would have been able to with any other experimental drug with human trials. They were encouraging people to use the extra time to travel or visit relatives. Schedules with regular ports of call, made overnight shipping of his drugs to the boat relatively easy. He asked me to come by his house every few days to check on his boarders and make sure no one was dead or tearing the place up.

He took very little with him on the ship. He didn't think he'd be able to do more than a few countries before having to return to die at home. I started getting post cards from ports of call in the Caribbean, and then Panama as his ship went through the Canal. Eventually it seemed as if he covered most of Asia. About 8 months later, I got a phone call from him. He was back home, and in the hospital. He wanted to see me.

During those years I made a lot of trips to hospitals to visit dying young men. Thankfully, I never got used to it. He had gotten sick and flown home. Now he wanted to get his final affairs in order. He wanted to sign a power of attorney to allow his realtor to sell his house. He figured that when he left the hospital, it would be to an AIDS hospice. His doctor was going to try him on something new, but we had all come to know when things were at the end.

I helped his tenants find other places to live. His realtor had placed his house on the market. It was a special place, so it was going to take some time to find the right buyer. I left that in his hands, and resigned myself to the phone call that always came. Instead, I got a different call. Six months after my last visit to him in the hospital, I got a call from him to meet him at his house. I wondered what could have happened.

Outside, there was a large moving van. Apparently, the new owners were moving in. I walked past a couple of guys carrying boxes in, and entered the living room. Tony was sitting on a stack of four boxes in the middle of the empty room. He looked well, robust even. He had put on weight, and he had very good color. The large Kaposi's scar I had gotten used to seeing on his cheek, like some kind of evil birth mark, was gone.

The new drug regimen that his doctor had put him on had worked. Nowadays we know it as the triple cocktail. Tony was one of the first people to be placed on it, and he had obviously responded well. Although he looked well, he also looked crestfallen. When he saw me he said, "I had everything well planned for dying. What am I supposed to do now that I'm going to live?" All I could say was "live." Then we both started laughing like we had just seen some absurd skit on Monte Python.

I thought he'd be really upset at losing the house he had put so much of himself into. In the scheme of things though, he didn't seem to mind. It had been a part of the past that was now gone in favor of an uncertain future. He still didn't know how long the new medicine would work for him. He didn't know if it would give him months, or years. We loaded his boxes up in my car, and I dropped him off at a friend's house. I didn't know when I might hear from him again.

About a year later, he called to say he was being sued. When he came by my office, he still looked great. He was being sued by the investment company that bought his life insurance. They were claiming that he and his doctor had lied about his terminal condition. I didn't really like these viatical companies, but they were useful for those who had no other options. They basically receive a 50% return on their investment in a year or two. Preying on people who are dying is kind of sleazy. When someone doesn't die, they get pretty bent out of shape. We're supposed to rejoice when someone has their cancer go into remission or receives a heart transplant. They don't.

We eventually settled with the company for a fraction of the money they wanted. Tony didn't mind; he had received a nice profit on the sale of his house. Since I saw him last, he'd gone to work at an architectural firm that designed homes for the disabled. He was afraid to open up a new solo office in case he became ill again. He didn't want to leave anyone in the lurch. Eventually he bought another house to fix up, and he made a life out of bringing historic but run down beauties back to life. He said everything deserved a second chance at life.

It took him about 8 years to accept the idea that he was going to live. He had continued to live his life, expecting to get sick and die at any moment. He didn't want to get into relationships for fear of what his dying would mean to him. Once over lunch he told me a story about the movie "The Big Red One." It followed a group of soldiers through World War II, and at some point they stopped wanting to get close to replacement soldiers. They were close to the original members of their platoon, but stayed at arm's length from new guys. Fear of the pain of loss was their constant companion.

When he finally accepted that he was going to live, he began to date again. Eventually he got married, and even had a child. There was a time when he went through a bad case of survivor's guilt. So many had died, but he had lived. Understanding why was the hard part. Believers would say it was God's will, that it was something that we aren't capable of understanding. Non-believers would say it was simply chance or his genetics that allowed him to live where so many others died. I like to think that God simply had something important he wanted Tony to do. He certainly taught me that second chances can be sweet.

JEAN

The longer I dealt with the mentally ill, especially those who had chemical dependency issues, the more it became clear to me that this stuff doesn't come out of thin air. When someone has been on the street for many years, they often have addiction issues. Sometimes their addictions put them on the streets, and sometimes being on the street has caused them to turn to chemicals to endure. Those with mental illnesses were often turning to street drugs or alcohol in order to self-medicate. It was an ultimate chicken or the egg scenario. I, too, have seen more than my share of broken people. Having come from a loving home, with a stay at home mother and a father who had a full time and stable job, if not low-paying, I had no idea that there were people in our society that came from abusive or neglectful homes.

As the youngest, and only girl, I naturally dealt with my fair share of teasing. I was not subjected to physical violence or sexual assault though. When I began to meet people who had been subjected to these things as children, experiences that I couldn't even imagine, I truthfully didn't know how to help them. One woman in particularly, though, stands out. She was my age, and we had gone to kindergarten together. She never met her father; her mother was an alcoholic who went from boyfriend to boyfriend. Many of them were violent drunks, and a couple were sexual predators. By the time I was getting ready for high school, she was working as a prostitute.

When we met again, she was addicted to heroin, suffering from AIDS, and weighed about 80 pounds. When I asked her what I could do to help her, she told me she wanted to die clean and sober. All her previous rehab attempts ended because as soon as she got the drugs out of her system, all she could think of was her past. All the episodes of abuse she had endured ran through her mind like a mini movie projector. The drugs stopped the memories.

I knew to stay sober, she would have to deal with her past. I had absolutely no idea how to access the help she needed. There was one thing I prided myself on, and that was I never lied to my clients. If I didn't know the answer to a question, I told them I didn't know, but would find out. Many lawyers would bluff their way through rather than admit they didn't know something. I told her to take care of her basic drug needs, while I found out who could help her. I made her promise to not share needles, and not to disappear. Sometimes when confronted with the idea of sobriety, clients would disappear rather than confront their demons.

My first call was to a nun I knew who worked at the woman's penitentiary. I figured that she would know someone who dealt with survivors of sexual abuse, as the rates of female abuse survivors in the criminal justice system are pretty high. She recommended a therapist who was a former nun, who was herself an abuse survivor and a recovering alcoholic. Jean had joined the convent as a young woman to escape her home situation and became an alcoholic to keep her demons at bay. Eventually she couldn't hide it anymore, and had to confront it. She got sober, left the convent, and went back to college to train to be a therapist to help others like herself. She risked every dime she could to open her own alcoholic counseling clinic.

Jean helped my former classmate heal, and she got her wish. She died clean and sober, and at peace for the first time in her life with Jean and I at her bedside. After that, I tried to repay Jean by helping her out. I helped her with her incorporation process, re-negotiated her office lease, and generally cleaned up the paperwork for her business. She had never done basic things like having a checking account or paying taxes until she had left the convent as a middle aged woman. Again, I thought to myself, I've got my work cut out for me.

She had lots of energy, but no real business experience. Once I got all the paperwork cleaned up, I started working on marketing. She had a habit of doing intensive therapy with clients who could not pay. As someone who routinely did the same thing, I completely understood. The difference is that I had a day job that covered my living expenses, and received a payment from the government with every successful disability filing I completed. She didn't. So, I negotiated a contract for her to teach traffic school classes for those who had been convicted of driving under the influence of drugs or alcohol. She began to run weekend seminars for adult survivors and the adult children of alcoholics.

There were lots of 12 step groups for a variety of conditions, including sex abuse survivors. Every time I thought I had heard the worst story yet, I would be confronted with even worse stories. Hearing the things that humans can do to each other is bad enough when dealing with adults, but hearing the things people had endured as children started to rattle me a bit. After about a year and a half, I started hearing even stranger stories. I heard people talking about their parents having been Satanists. I had traveled all over Oklahoma, and I had met nothing but good people in most of the small towns I went to while working with farmers. The idea that some of them could be Satanists, just pushed me over a line into incredulity.

That's when I began to question some of the therapeutic practices Jean was involved in. Other than college psychology classes, experience as a mediator, and common sense, I had no training as a therapist. One of her mentors was a former Jesuit priest. He was qualified to do pastoral counseling, but I found out that he was involved in hypnotizing clients, and teaching other therapists to do the same. That really troubled me. I knew how hypnosis could be used to help witnesses remember crimes, and that testimony elicited that way wasn't allowed in court. It is too easy to manipulate people into remembering what you want them to. I found out that many of Jean's patients were now convinced they had multiple personality disorder and had recovered memories of things happening to them as children. She had a college degree in human resources and was trained to help alcoholics. She wasn't a psychiatrist, or even a psychologist.

When I confronted her with my concerns, she made me read a book about childhood sexual assault. The main theme of this self-help book was that if you have the symptoms of having been abused, then you must have been, and you just don't remember it yet. The fact that there are lots of conditions that can manifest in those same symptoms without a history of abuse was apparently not important to the authors. I felt I had a fiduciary responsibility to help Jean see that she was placing herself, and her business, at legal risk by offering a type of therapy that she had no real training in, nor certification to use. There are times as an attorney where clients will simply refuse to listen to any advice you have.

When confronted with a stubborn client, you have two choices. You can fire them as a client and move on, or you can continue to work with them, so long as you are firm with them that they are acting against legal advice. As I was pondering what I wanted to do, several things occurred that made my mind up for me. First, I found out Jean had again been refusing to ask clients for payment. She was financing her personal expenses by switching debt around to a group of over-extended credit cards. Additionally, to try to make up the difference, she had been gambling every evening and all day on weekends at bingo halls. She had also been selling stock in her business to friends and family members. This violated securities regulations.

I had decided to look at her financial issues as just another addiction she had fallen into, but then I got notice about one of her clients that really troubled me. I had helped this couple incorporate a small business. The husband had come up with an idea for a new type of fishing lure to use in murky water. I thought it was a really good idea, and I helped him find a student at the community college who was going to help him get a proto-type out. He had even gotten mentioned on a national fishing show. What I didn't find out until later is that after that spot aired on TV, he had placed an ad for the lure in a national fishing magazine, and was getting orders. The problem was, he hadn't followed through on the prototype or any kind of production, and had spent all the money people had sent him, and had also been selling stock in his company. Jean had shown him how.

That was the last straw. I couldn't ethically continue to represent clients who were going to commit fraud. My good name was worth more to me than that. I was willing to help them make things right, but neither wanted to do the hard work that would require. Jean kept expecting to win big at bingo to solve her problems, and her fisherman client kept thinking someone was going to buy the idea from him for millions and fill his orders. I learned a valuable lesson. When someone has an addictive personality, just because they are no longer drinking or using drugs, doesn't mean they aren't still deep in addictive thinking. Jean had simply traded alcohol for gambling. The real losers, besides their stockholders, were her clients. They came to her broken, and because she wasn't whole herself, they left even more broken.

Years later, the "recovered memory" people had mostly been discredited. Jean's clients had all moved on to more qualified professionals to clean up the mess she had made of their lives. Some of their parents, who had wrongly been accused of horrific acts, had died before their names could be cleared. I sometimes think about how hard it must be to be falsely accused of something so devastating, and wonder if their families were ever able to recover. The fisherman ended up in jail for a variety of financial crimes. I got a call from him in jail, and had to tell him that I couldn't represent him. Jean ended up losing her business, and her home. Last I heard she was working at the state mental hospital as an attendant on the night shift. Her stockholders never pressed charges. One elderly woman, who had given her most of her retirement money, had a stroke.

What I learned from Jean is that abuse has a way of echoing. Those who have been hurt often go on to hurt others. Healthy people don't hurt people, only hurting ones do. Making sure that people receive proper and timely care can put a stop to an infection. It's hard to imagine dysfunction and abuse as being like an infection, but that is the way it spreads.

HIDDEN DEMONS

My disability is mostly visible. My head injury isn't, but seeing crutches or a walker immediately tells people that I've got something wrong. There were two women I met at the counseling center whose issues were decidedly hidden. The counseling center allowed 12 step groups to use the facilities on off evenings. It was kind of an outreach and marketing program combined. One of these was a group for bulimics and anorexics, and most of the people who attended those meetings were young females. I saw a middle aged woman once, and assumed she had come to support her daughter. Her name was Theresa.

After talking to her, she admitted that she was a bulimic and had been for decades. Her mother and grandmother were both overweight. She was as well in grade school, but someone had told her about eating and then throwing up, and she hated herself so much that she gave it a try. When she started losing weight, she was hooked. Thus began a lifetime of hiding. She learned how to cover the sound of her vomiting in public restrooms. She learned how to cover the sound at home. She devised a thousand lies to explain why she needed to leave the table immediately after eating.

After a time she learned all the tricks. She would use "marker" foods, which was something like a cheeto or carrot that was a bright color, and she would eat this first so that she would know when she had reached the end of her need to purge. She discovered which foods came up easiest, and which left the smallest aftertaste. She also began to experience side effects; she had constant heart burn. She joked once that at a certain point in her teen years that her main source of calories was antacids because those she didn't throw back up. At times she could go without purging for weeks, but every time she encountered stress in her life, or a feeling that she wasn't in control, she purged again. It became the one thing in her life she felt like she had complete control over. It allowed her to fill her stomach, but rid herself of it before it made her gain weight. At least when she felt full, she felt something.

She would occasionally pass out in the heat of Oklahoma summers because she was dehydrated and her electrolytes were being depleted. Her parents had doctors run all sorts of tests on her out of fear she had some kind of horrible disease. Doctors at that time didn't know what to look for. She developed ulcers, and her parents contacted her teachers asking them to not put too much pressure on her. When her dentist found wounds in her mouth from her fingers, he assumed she was gritting her teeth in her sleep and prescribed a dental mouth guard.

After she married, and they had difficulty conceiving a child, she finally admitted to her family doctor that she had been purging for years. He was stunned. He didn't believe her at first. Once he got over the shock, he explained to her that not being able to conceive was going to be the least of her worries. He wanted to tell her husband, but she refused to give him permission. She promised to quit, and did long enough to become pregnant. As she gained weight with the pregnancy, she began to panic. She started purging again, and had a miscarriage.

She was afraid to tell her husband what she had done. She was determined to stop this time, and did long enough to have a healthy baby. She gained 75 pounds during the pregnancy. She began to purge again immediately after giving birth, and lost that weight in short order, but was unable to nurse her new baby. Her husband believed it was just one of those things, and didn't think anything more about it. Her quick weight loss led to another round of her passing out. Once she fainted while holding her new baby. Their baby was unharmed, but she became very careful while holding her baby after that. Her husband thought it was happening because of lack of sleep from caring for a new baby.

She was very careful with the amount of food she fed the baby. She didn't want her daughter to fall into the same trap she had. The baby wasn't developing normally. When her doctor realized what was happening, he threatened her with social service involvement unless she told her husband about her eating disorder. He was equally stunned and disgusted. He almost divorced her, but was afraid of losing custody of his daughter. They went into therapy, and she was able to keep her illness under control or at least under wraps for the next 20 years. She couldn't hide the damage done to her teeth. Purging causes acid erosion on the back of your teeth.

When her husband questioned the amount of money the dentist was charging to cap most of her teeth, she blamed it on damage from years before. He seemed suspicious, but mollified. When her hair began to fall out, she blamed her genes. She was treated for repeated yeast infections, caused by her sugar binges. Her husband just thought that was an ordinary woman kind of thing. Shortly after their 20th wedding anniversary, she began to spit up blood. Alarmed, she ended up in the ER where it was discovered that she had a rupture in the wall of her esophagus. He overheard the doctor discussing her bulimia, and realized she had continued to binge and purge off and on for years. A year later, after their daughter went off to college, he left his wife for another woman. Apparently she wasn't the only one keeping secrets in the marriage.

Her divorce sent her into a horrible spiral. Her weight plunged drama-tically. Her daughter talked her into going to long term treatment, where she found herself surrounded by high school and college aged girls that she had little in common with, except binging and purging. She had periods of recovery, but every time some life issue came up, she fell back into her disorder. After a job loss sent her into a spiral of depression, her weight got so frighteningly low that her daughter had her involuntarily committed to treatment. The only thing she really felt was self-loathing. Years passed, and her daughter married and began to have a family of her own. Seeing her grandchildren made her realize she actually had something worth living for. She made a real effort in therapy to discover the source of her illness, and had been abstinent, their version of sobriety, for several years when I met her. She never missed a meeting. She still felt out of place among the young women, but felt like she gave them something important, a view of their future if they don't get help for their illnesses. She said it was important because most who are as sick as she had become simply do not reach middle age.

The other woman who struck me during this time was Janet. She had come in wearing long sleeve shirts on a very hot day. When we began to talk, she was very open by the fact that she was here because she was trying to stay alive. She was a member of a group for the adult survivors of child abuse. Her long sleeves covered the damage she had done to her forearms and wrists with repeated suicide attempts. In my mind, I imagined scars that might look like red marks on her skin. Instead her forearms looked like they had been put into a garbage disposal. They were ridged and had deep crevasses that ran from wrist to elbow, in places it looked like the skin of someone who had been badly burned. I didn't wonder at how she had ended up that way, but how she had survived inflicting that much damage on herself. I had dealt with women who had small scratch marks on their wrists from half-hearted suicide attempts that were just cries for help. Janet had meant business with her attempts.

She was hoping to eventually have some reconstructive surgery and skin grafts to make her arms look more normal. Her doctors were refusing until she had gone a certain length of time without another suicide attempt. She was also working to raise the money she would need for the surgery since her insurance company refused to pay. They considered it to be purely cosmetic. I asked a stupid question, wanting to know if it hurt. She had done so much nerve damage that she really didn't have feeling in her arms. She said she didn't mind being asked. In fact, most people are too aghast to ask any questions at all and pretend that they can't see the damage. She said my curiosity was normal, and by asking, I was treating her as a normal person as well, rather than some kind of lunatic that needed to be ignored and avoided.

To stay alive, she also had to get to the root of the emotional issues that made her feel like killing herself. She had been abused as a child. Her mother was the primary wage earner of the family, and she worked many hours as a loan officer at a bank. Her father was a salesman who had worked at almost every car dealer and furniture store in town. He rarely kept a job for more than a few months at a time. He was the one who got Theresa up for school, and was there when she came home from school. He had begun abusing her shortly after she entered the third grade. He had a drinking problem which led to his serial unemployment. Between jobs, he spent more time at home and had more free time to abuse his daughter in a drunken stupor.

Her first suicide attempt came shortly after her 12th birthday. That was right after her father had graduated from fondling, to rape. She told me that she figured death was better than staying around to be abused again. Her first attempt had gone horizontally across her wrists. She said she had to cut through too many tendons and such in order to get to the artery. She was easily saved that time, but learned from the doctor how lucky she was that she hadn't cut her arms vertically, because she would have certainly died that way. Instead of being relieved, she was grateful to the doctor for telling her how to be successful the next time she wanted to attempt it.

She was committed to a juvenile facility for some time after her first attempt. Everyone there was miserable and looking for a way to get out. To her it was like a vacation, and she never wanted to leave to go back to her father. Her mother refused to attempt family counseling. She considered the entire episode as an embarrassment and was convinced her daughter hadn't really known what she was attempting to do. She put the whole thing down to one of those stupid things kids sometimes do. Her father knew differently, and promised her that things would be different when she came home. He also told her that if she told the doctors that she had done it because he had been abusing her, they would put her in juvenile hall.

She took him at his word, and never broke her silence. Eventually after three months, she was deemed cured and released back to her parents. Her father left her alone for many months, but after a nasty holiday fight where her mother decided to go out of town to a business meeting around Christmas rather than stay home with her family, her father got really drunk, and the abuse began anew. It went on for a couple of years before she felt like she couldn't take any more. Before her second suicide attempt, she had broken down and told her mother what was going on at home while she was at work. She expected her very forceful, professional mother to put a stop to it. Instead, she was punished for telling the truth. Her mother didn't believe her. She felt like something inside her had died. That time, she cut her wrists vertically. It took hundreds of stitches to save her life. Had her father not been sent home from work early that day for getting drunk during lunch, she would have died.

She found herself in a state facility this time. Her mother decided that sending her to the nice private juvenile facility was a waste of money. She was surrounded by teens that set fires and mutilated cats. She broke down in a therapy session and admitted to her father's abuse. The police were informed, and her father was brought in for questioning. Her mother told the police that her daughter was a liar who was making the allegations to get back at her parents for not allowing her to date. Her mother was important enough that the police didn't want to file charges without some solid evidence. The entire case was dropped. Her mother was so mad at her that she signed her over to be a ward of the state. When she was finally released from the hospital, she went to a group home that was one step above a place for juvenile delinquents. While she no longer had to worry about her father assaulting her, she did have to worry about being assaulted by other inmates and staff.

By the time she was 18, she felt like she had nothing to live for. She had no family, no diploma, and had spent the last three years of her life being in almost daily abuse. She said she watched a movie about concentration camp survivors, and the women had the same look in their eyes that she saw every time she looked into a mirror. The next ten years she worked as a sex trade worker, and was repeatedly hospitalized after suicide attempts. Finally during her last hospitalization, she had a female psychiatrist who was willing to work with her on a personal level. It was the first time she had mentioned her childhood abuse since the first time. She arranged for Theresa to go to a group home for women trying to get out of the sex trades, and she went to work as a cleaner in a large hotel near the group home.

What I found most interesting about Theresa is that she never used drugs. I'd never met a clean prostitute before. She explained that most prostitutes use drugs to deaden themselves to the life of degradation they had found themselves in. She hated herself so much that she wanted to feel every abuse the John's and Joe's wanted to inflict on her. My mother had worked as a housecleaner in her grandfather's motel, and her stories had made me convinced I never wanted to do that job. I asked her how she stood doing the job. She actually loved it. It was the idea that no matter how dirty someone left something, she could make it clean. She could make it look like new, and she felt that each room she cleaned made her soul a bit cleaner too.

Ultimately, what Janet and Theresa taught me is that we can hide our invisible disabilities from everyone except ourselves. I have no idea if either woman was able to continue their recovery, or fell back into a life of dysfunction and disorder. What I learned though, is that we never truly fail so long as we don't give up. If we have a slip, so long as we continue to get up, dust ourselves off, and start again, we haven't failed. We may just not have completely succeeded yet. For most, recovery isn't a destination to reach, it is life long journey.

AND DO CALL ME SHIRLEY

Because I had the reputation of being willing to take on clients who had AIDS, I started to have many clients unlike anyone I had ever met in my middle class neighborhood. One is still very vivid in my mind. He was 6'3" tall, rather rough and pasty looking, and was wearing high heels and a bright red dress the day I met him. He walked in, shook my hand, and introduced himself as Shirley. Once again, I had to make a split second decision to keep a straight face and hope that someone wasn't playing a practical joke on me.

I knew that there was no way that this man had been born with the name Shirley, and I could have made a fuss about it, but decided to just take this man where he was. I'm very glad I did. I think he expected me to send him away, make fun of him, or even respond in disgust. I tried to focus on his eyes so that the rest of him would be out of sight, so to speak. When I asked him what I could do to help him, he just sat in the chair and cried.

He eventually told me the story of his life. He had always been different. As a child, he preferred to play with his sisters' dolls. He liked helping his mother with the cooking and laundry. His mother knew he was different and tried to protect him, but his father hated him. He had wanted a son to play catch with and go to ball games with. Instead he had been given a son who didn't care for sports. His father made fun of him, beat him up in the misguided attempt to toughen him up, and eventually began to abuse him. His father threatened to emasculate him since he wanted to be a girl anyway. By the time he was a teenager, he began to use drugs to deaden the pain he was feeling, and his father kicked him out of the house.

He took a job butchering chickens. He slept in the back of the facility. Although he was surrounded with blood and smell of death, he actually felt free for the first time in his life. When he was old enough, he joined the army. He spent several tours of duty in Southeast Asia, where he was exposed to all the sexual delights he could possibly want. This experimentation far surpassed anything he experienced experimenting with drugs. He had found a new drug. When he came home, he began driving a cross country truck route. He knew every brothel or prostitute strip in every town large enough to have a gas station.

He said all the time he was having sex with women, it was as if he was trying to prove to himself that he was a man, to prove his father wrong. The more he tried, the worse he felt, and eventually he went back to using drugs to dull the pain. One winter while driving under the influence of drugs, he crashed his truck into an embankment, and broke many bones including most of the bones in his face. During his hospitalization, when the plastic surgeon discussed with him how they were going to repair his face, he was shown a book of cheeks and noses to help the doctor understand how he wanted his repaired face to look. He realized that every face that appealed to him belonged to a female. The plastic surgeon did too, and asked for a psychiatric consult.

For the first time in his life, this man was talking about how he felt rather than trying to run away from it. After more than a year of seeing this psychiatrist, he was finally able to admit to himself that he truly wanted to be a woman. He began the process of getting approved for sexual re-assignment surgery. One of the conditions was that he had to begin to live his life for at least a year as a female before the surgery could be done. The trucking industry at that time actually had many homosexual drivers, but they were lesbians, not transsexuals. The first day he arrived to drive a truck wearing a dress, he was fired.

I was being asked to argue his case for receiving unemployment. He didn't just want me to prove that he had been fired without just cause, he wanted me to prove that the transport company had discriminated against him. I had successfully argued several cases before administrative judges at the Employment Security Commission. All of those had been where the employee had quit due to the employer having a hostile work environment. Often, employers wouldn't fire someone who had AIDS outright, but rather made it so difficult or abusive to continue working there that my clients had quit. Normally if you quit your job, you aren't entitled to unemployment benefits. Shirley's employer had actually fired him, for cause. The cause was that he had been late for work. He hadn't been, but this is also a tactic unscrupulous employers use to avoid having to pay unemployment benefits.

There was, at that time, absolutely no protections against firing someone based on sexual orientation. There were, however, laws against discriminating in the workplace based on gender. I made the argument that his sexual orientation had nothing to do with the termination because the company employed several known homosexuals. I made the argument that he was instead discriminated based on gender. Had he been a gay woman, he would not have been fired. He was fired because he was a man, and that is discrimination based on gender.

The administrative judge looked at me with a puzzled look on her face for several minutes. She then called a recess, excused herself to her chambers, and didn't return for two hours. When she did, without an explanation, she awarded my client his benefits, fined his former employer for false statements, and suggested that we file a complaint against the employer with the Human Rights Commission. I had already done so, and ultimately, he agreed to pay my client a nice settlement rather than go through with the publicity that the human rights complaint would bring.

Shirley celebrated his settlement by deciding to buy himself an entire wardrobe. He asked me to accompany him to the store to get a second opinion. Few women turn down the opportunity to go clothes shopping, but I was not sure if I wanted to be seen in public trying on clothes with a transsexual. He told me to meet him behind a well-known big and tall ladies clothing store at midnight. I've always been tall, and have laughably prominent feet, so this was one of my favorite shops. I'd never shopped there at midnight though.

When I arrived, I found the alley behind the store full of cars, and a security guard standing at the back supply entrance. The security guard gave us a long look, and then let us inside. The atmosphere was like a sorority house party. There were about two dozen men running around the place in a variety of stages of being dressed or undressed. Shirley began running around trying things on with the rest of the crowd and quickly forgot I was there. It was like being in a really strange movie.

I mostly tried to stay out of the way. I went towards the front of the store and saw that the curtains had been drawn. The owner of the shop was an older woman that always reminded me a bit of my grandmother. When she saw me, she was alarmed, and started stammering apologies about the "disturbance." Once I explained to her that I was here with a client, and not to shop, she relaxed. It turned out that these midnight madness events had been started years before by her deceased husband. In the beginning, he told her that he stayed late at the shop once a month to do inventory. She became a bit suspicious that he never wanted her to help him.

One night, she decided to drive to the shop to see if he was actually there. She had been afraid that he was seeing another woman. She walked in on a scene very much like the one that was occurring presently. Her husband explained that he would catch men coming in to try on clothing surreptitiously and it upset other customers who found them in the changing rooms. He started these nights to give the local drag queens and transsexuals a safe place to try on clothes. It made the store a nice extra profit, and kept the guys from disturbing his day-time female clientele.

After her husband passed away, she continued the practice. This was in a time before the internet existed and finding a local source for size 14 red leather stilettos was next to impossible. The guys trying on clothes were having such a good time it was impossible to not join in the fun. My surgically reconstructed ankle would never allow me to wear a six inch heel, but we had a great deal of fun playing with the feathered boas. It was the one place where they could be themselves in a town where men were supposed to wear cowboy boots.

At the end of the evening, they put everything that wasn't being purchased back neatly where it belonged. The cash register binged like a pinball machine with all the purchases, and Shirley had an entire wardrobe to begin his new life. He took a job selling makeup for a well-known national company. He would do make overs for men in the privacy of their homes. He won many sales contests that usually resulted in prizes of vacations or cruises. I got postcards from all sorts of exotic locations. He completed his surgery and returned to my office for a legal name change.

Shirley taught me a lot of things about meeting people where they are. He also taught me that we can't hide from our past, and we can't hide who we really are inside for long without doing damage. At our first meeting, I told him that my personal faith told me that having sexual reassignment wasn't part of God's plan for us. He thought that meant that I wouldn't represent him. I had many clients over the years that I couldn't understand or condone the way they were living their lives. That doesn't mean that they aren't entitled to proper representation.

Every human is of equal dignity. Just because I don't understand why God gives some people such heavy crosses, doesn't mean that he has made a mistake. God doesn't make mistakes. Shirley was as much a part of God's creation as I was. Perhaps Shirley was God's way of teaching me compassion for those most disenfranchised by our society. He certainly taught me many things, including never making assumptions based on first impressions. He also taught me how to blend foundations and cover-ups to perfectly work with my very ruddy complexion. That came in handy in a few short months when I had to learn to cover up scars.

WHO AM I

I didn't set out to have a legal career revolving around those most stig-
matized. I just didn't turn them away when they came through my door.
I couldn't imagine that anyone would, but found out that wasn't the case.
Of course, once I helped one vulnerable person, the grapevine buzzed
that I would handle things out of the ordinary. Chris certainly fell into
that category.

She walked in, and sat down. She didn't seem to be capable of speaking
for a few minutes, but I was used to this. By the time people found my
door, they had lived with secrets for so long that they no longer knew
how to be open. Eventually she said, "I don't know what gender I am."
I was relieved that it was something relatively simple, or at least, I
thought so. I told her that I had experience dealing with transgendered
individuals, and not to worry, I'd help her.

She was silent for a bit longer, and then told me that I didn't understand.
She wasn't a woman trapped in a man's body or vice versa. She literally
did not know if she was born as a male or a female. I'm rarely at a loss
for words, but this took a minute to sink in. Pictures of neutered GI
Joes went through my mind, and I shook my head to clear them. I was
reminded that law school hadn't prepared me for this client. Nothing had.

Before me was a 40 year old person who had lived her entire life not knowing what gender she was born with. She had never allowed herself to be
seen in a gymnasium shower or locker room. She had never dated or

gone to the doctor. She had lived in fear of discovery. Her birth certif-
icate said female, but her parents told her that the doctor told them he
wasn't sure. Her parents were terrified that their secret would be found
out that they relocated to another state. They had been older when she
was born and always blamed themselves for not having children when
they were younger.

She never had normal experiences growing up. She was never left with
a babysitter, out of fear they might have to change her diaper. She
never went to sleepovers. She never visited her grandparents for the
summer. She never entered a public swimming pool. She never played
on a sports team. She was afraid to have close friends. Her parents
were afraid to have another child, for fear that it was genetic and they
would have another one like her. Her only friends growing up were her
pets. She knew her parents loved her, but she always felt like she had
ruined their lives.

She had spent her life driving a long haul truck. She slept in the back,
and tried to sign up for different routes each trip so that she wouldn't
have to deal with the same truck stops, the same warehouse workers,
or even the same roads. She lived in fear of having an accident and waking
up in the emergency room where they had discovered her secret. She
spent Christmas and Thanksgiving with her parents. They had always
referred to her as female, and raised her as such for a relatively simple
reason. They thought that as a female she would have more privacy in
public bathrooms. They also thought that society was easier of women
viewed as tom boys than on men viewed as too feminine.

She had thought many times over the years about trying to have some
surgery to make herself look more normal, but didn't want it to become
public and embarrass her parents. Her parents were now both deceased,
and she thought it was time. She started to describe what her genitals
looked like, but I told her I didn't need to know to help her. She insisted;
it was as if she had to. She had spent her entire life hiding, and now that
she had found the courage to confront it, she needed to tell someone,
anyone, in order to not chicken out and run away to hide again.

As she described her physical oddity, I tried very hard not to blink or look too shocked. When she was finished, she put her face in her hands. I took a deep breath, and asked her if she was okay. She said no, had never been, but hoped she was making the right decision. I told her our first step was a doctor. I had no idea what kind though, and admitted it. With her permission, I called my doctor, and discussed it with her over the phone. I'm glad it wasn't on speakerphone because the first thing my doctor said was that she was too busy for one of my pranks. When she realized I wasn't joking, she agreed to see Chris that afternoon.

I have never really liked going to doctors. I've had so many orthopedic surgeries that I'm afraid every time I go in that the doctor is going to want to cut on me again. So I knew that if I sent Chris off by herself, she might make a run for it. It was a long wait sitting in the waiting room, pretending to read dated magazines, but just flipping the pages looking at the pictures. I was terrified that she would ask me to come into the examination room with her, but she didn't. She walked to the back when the nurse called her name, with her shoulders hunched over, shuffling her feet. It reminded me of someone going to the gallows.

It was about 45 minutes later that I was asked to come back to my doctor's office. Chris was sitting there, and my doctor said that she had requested I hear her conclusions. She had diagnosed her condition as indeterminate gender. It is also referred to as being intersexed. There are several different things that can cause it, either genetic or in vitro issues. In either case, her next step was to undergo genetic testing first to see exactly what we were dealing with. She did tell Chris that no matter what was discovered as the cause of her condition, it wouldn't change how she felt about herself. If she felt like a woman or a man, that probably wouldn't miraculously change. Doctors could make her plumbing look more normal, but that wasn't going to change what her brain thought.

It took about a month to get into the geneticist and begin having some specialized blood work done. This was the first time in over 20 years that Chris had been in the same place for any length of time. She spent her days doing things like visiting the zoo and going to movies. I knew she was trying to fill every minute of the wait so she didn't have to think too much. A couple of weeks in, I discovered there was a local support group for intersexed individuals. I suggest she try going to a meeting, but she didn't want to. I thought maybe she was afraid or too nervous, but it wasn't that at all. She simply wanted to be able to tell the other people like her what she really was first.

I did talk to the parents of an intersexed child, and they said that in the delivery room when they asked the doctor if it was a boy or girl, he hesitated and said, "Um, give me a minute." These births happen in about 1 out of every 2,000 births, and many believe that the rate is increasing. There was a time when parents and doctors chose a gender and performed surgery to make the infant's genitalia match that choice. Today, it is deemed better to allow the child to eventually decide for themselves, and surgery is only done if there is an issue with proper urination. Many adult individuals are scarred by the quick decision surgery done to them as infants. At least Chris had not dealt with those issues. In many jurisdictions, it is now possible to check a third box as gender rather than just male or female.

Chris ultimately discovered that she was female, and decided to have some corrective surgery. The surgery itself wasn't that invasive or difficult, and she finally went through a great deal of long overdue therapy. She was faced with having to accept that her parents never had it done to save themselves from embarrassment. They had hidden her not for her benefit, but for their own benefit. Her recovery is ongoing, but she made huge strides in her personal life. She gave up long haul driving, and settled down to a job teaching others to drive big rigs. Her fear of having an accident had made her a very safe driver over the years.

She bought a small house and decorated it with lots of lace inside, and a well-equipped man cave garage on the outside. Instead of trying to settle into a gender defined role, she embraced her diversity. She eventually married someone from her intersexed support group. The pronoun issues would have driven me a bit batty, but she had lived her entire life living those issues, so it seemed normal to her. I was really happy for her. She had carried a hidden burden for so long that any life lived in the sunshine had to be incredible.

I dealt with one other intersexed individual in my career. His story was just as sad, but had a vastly different outcome. Tom had been born with normal genitalia, however, when he was a few days old, his circumcision went badly. Gangrene set into his penis, and it had to be removed. I can't imagine what his parents must have gone through when this happened, so I don't have the same harsh feelings for them that Tom developed.

At the urging of their physician, they decided to put Tom through gender reassignment surgery to make him a female. He grew up being treated as a female, but he said, as I have heard many transgendered people say, that he just didn't feel right. He wanted to be rough and tumble, not delicate and demure. He grew up knowing that he was born with a strange illness that caused a vitamin deficiency. His doctors prescribed special vitamins, and those vitamins were significantly increased when he entered puberty. He did wonder why he wasn't starting to have periods like his other female friends. At first he was told that he was just a late bloomer. Later his parents told him it was part of the disease he was born with. They didn't know if he would ever be able to be a mother.

To an ordinary female, this prognosis would have been devastated. Tom said he almost felt relief, which again he felt was odd. He also didn't feel right dating males in high school. He knew he should, but began to think that he must be gay, and that explained all the strange feelings he had growing up. On his 18th birthday, after the party goers had all departed, his parents said they needed to have a long talk with him. They said they had hoped this day would never come. Tom's original physician had retired, and the younger doctor who had taken over his practice had told them that he would not go along with their subterfuge once he had reached adulthood.

He heard the whole story about his injury, his surgery, and that the vitamins he had taken all his life were in fact female hormones to allow his body to develop as a female. He was devastated. He had been lied to. He had been drugged without his knowledge and his very identity had been stolen by the people he had trusted the most, his parents. He wanted to kill them. He wanted to kill himself. He spent the next several months suing everyone involved.

By the time I met him 10 years later, he had legally changed his name and received large sums of money from the hospital and the doctor who performed his surgery, and the doctor who originally injured him. He had undergone hormone therapy, a double mastectomy, and reconstructive surgery. To all appearances, he was an ordinary male, but there was something about his eyes that seemed dead to me. He wanted me to help him get some privacy back in his life.

His parents would not leave him alone. He had moved a dozen times, and each time they had tracked him down. He never wanted to see them again or have to hear their voices, especially their apologies. He was also being tracked down by reporters for interviews. His parents had appeared on a local TV talk show and exposed all his history. He wanted to secure an injunction against his parents to prevent them from talking publicly about him again, and he wanted to legally change his name, but keep his new name sealed by the court.

I was about half way through his paperwork, when I was injured and was unable to finish his case. A friend of mine took over, and he received all his requests from the court. His parents had their attorney file a motion to force their son to attend the hearing in person. They wanted to force him to be in the same room with them. The judge turned down the motion, and said it was further evidence of why Tom needed the redress he was seeking. With his new name, he relocated again to another state.

A few years later, the attorney that had handled his case in my stead called me. Tom had committed suicide. The only reason he had been informed is that he had been contacted by Tom's current attorney for some inform- ation relating to his probate. I suppose there are some wounds that can never heal. I remember my mother and father talking about a neighbor's son who had come back from Vietnam with a severe injury to his pelvic area. He also eventually committed suicide. My dad said there were some things that you just couldn't get over. He said during his war, soldiers wouldn't have survived a wound like that, and maybe that was a blessing. What I learned from these two clients is that our gender and sense of sexuality are at the very core of our being. When something about that goes wrong, either in our head or in our body, it can be devastating.

THE WILD MAN

My actual day job was trying to keep family farmers on their farms. When the State Agriculture Department found out that the number one cause of death among farmers at the time was suicide, they decided that dealing with mental illness was worth their time. It was a pretty hard sell among Oklahoma farmers though. They all think they should be able to handle all their own problems.

My job wasn't to deal with their mental illnesses though. That was handled by a free hotline with a farmer's widow with a counseling degree on the other end of the line. We also set up group therapy centers in rural areas. My job was to handle their legal affairs, and to run a mediation program so they could negotiate with their creditors. Helping that end of their problems though, often helped their mental health.

I had a bad habit of staying late at work. Our in-house counselor made herself available almost 24 hours a day. She had lost her husband to a heart attack after they had lost their farm early in the farm crisis. Saving other farmers wasn't just her job, it was her vocation. At night, the hotline phones were forwarded to her home. When I worked late, the phone would ring once, and then shut off when it was forwarded.

One evening, the phone kept ringing. Our counselor had forgotten to forward the phones before leaving. I answered the phone somewhat irritated, only to hear a voice on the other end of the phone say, "I have a gun in my mouth." Nothing in law school had prepared me for this either. Without really thinking, I blurted out, "Isn't it hard to talk with a gun in your mouth?" After that ignominious beginning, I was able to talk him into putting the gun down. A few short minutes later, or hours later, I have no idea which, his wife came home from work and put the guns and ammunition away. He got admitted to a hospital and placed on some antidepressants, and survived his temporary insanity. That's what suicide is after all, a permanent solution to a temporary problem.

If law school hadn't prepared me for suicidal clients, it had also not prepared me for homicidal ones either. Sitting at my desk one day, I received a call from a representative of a bank that was going to be involved in a mediation hearing in a couple of weeks with one of our farmers. He asked me if we were going to have it in a courthouse where the farmer would have to go through a metal detector. I was pretty sure the small county courthouse didn't have one, and asked why he wanted to use one, a bit afraid of what his answer was going to be.

The farmer in question was the great-nephew of a very famous old western outlaw. He liked to remind everyone of his heritage by wearing a colt .45 on his hip, complete with pearled handles. He also used a rather unusual walking stick; he had taken a bullet in his hip during the D-Day landings in 1944. His sore hip was supported with the aid of an electric cattle prod. I can still see this larger than life man walking down the street, wearing old bib overalls, six shooter on his hip, and clunking along with that cattle prod. He had repelled every attempt to foreclose on his farm by scaring the local sheriff's deputies out of serving him the papers.

Mediation works best when both parties come together to work out their issues peaceably. The idea that this banker was asking me to ensure his safety in order to attend, seemed to me to be quite counter to the foundation of mediation. It was the only time that I decided to cancel a mediation. Instead, I had the farmer come into my office, and his creditors meet in this banker's office; we did a mediation by telephone. The farmer agreed to a new payment plan to get his farm back on track. He signed it, we faxed it, and the rest of his creditors signed it and faxed it back again.

Six months later, I got another call from the banker, and was told that this farmer hadn't made a single payment. He had begun to sell off equipment and animals that he'd taken out loans on, but refused to pay his creditors. The creditors had placed liens at the local stockyards, so the farmer had been taking his cows two counties over to sell. This had gone from a simple civil matter, to a criminal matter. The farmer didn't live long enough to see himself come before a judge like his famous ancestor had. He didn't live long enough to see the rest of his farm and equipment sold at auction. The stress of trying to hold onto a farm that he could no longer financially or physically manage, caused a heart attack. He was buried with his six shooter, and his boots on, like a true cowboy.

It was very difficult working with troubled farmers. They couldn't understand how the farm their grandfather's saved during the Great Depression, and their dad's saved during the war years, could now be lost from their hands. Sometimes the only way I could save the farmer, was for him to lose the farm. Many refused to give up without a fight. Once we got a call from a farmer's wife asking us to please get a hold of the county sheriff. Her husband had found out that the sheriff was coming to serve foreclosure documents on them. She said he had called in a bunch of his friends, and she had never seen so many army machine guns in her life. The sheriff was walking into an ambush. Our counselor started making calls, and found someone close by who was able to intercept the sheriff just in time.

Farmers are simple thinkers, not simpletons. They just do a really hard job the best way they can. They do the same things that farmers have done for 10 000 years, so when they run into trouble, it hard for them to understand why. They expect a drought or hail storm at the wrong time to hurt them, but there's always a next year for them to try again. The farm crisis of the 80's was different. It was made worse by droughts and floods, but at its heart was a change in global economies. Trying to explain that to a farmer with an 8th grade education was tough.

When times are bad, there are always those willing to take advantage of people's fears. Snake oil salesmen and flimflam men have always been with us. Those who traffic on fear and hate are the scariest, but we can all understand someone trying to make a dollar off someone who is desperate. We may despise them, but we at least know why they do what they do. The hatemongers confuse me to this day. Do they truly believe the hate they spew, or are they deluded? I suppose there are some of both kinds. One thing I do know is that children have to be taught to hate. We aren't born to hate. We are born to love, and some of us take the wrong path at some point in their lives.

Proverbs 9:7 says, "He who corrects a scoffer gets himself abuse, and he who reproves a wicked man incurs injury." As some would say, haters are going to hate. I wasn't raised to hate people because of the color of their skin or because of the country of their birth. I had known some discrimination because my family was poor or because we were Catholic in a place where that was rare. My Godparents, that I loved as if they were my own parents, were Mexican. When I heard people say derogatory things about Latinos, it wounded me. I never wanted to be one of those people.

When I was a junior in high school, the Ku Klux Klan recruited on my school grounds. I don't remember now why or how that happened. We had experienced a lot of racial tensions in my school, and several actual riots, especially after a white freshman was shot and killed by a black student right in the hallway. I walked up to the man, and he started his sales pitch. I have a typical Irish ruddy complexion, and I guess he thought he had an eager prospect. I let him talk for 15 minutes, and he wanted to get me to sign on the dotted line. As I was leaning over with a pen in my hand, I looked up and asked him if it mattered that I was Catholic. He turned almost as pale as the white sheet he was wearing. I tossed down his pen and walked away.

So years later when I saw that same man talking to one of my farmers at a rural meeting, I became incensed. White supremacists could offer something to my farmers that I couldn't, someone to blame. I could talk about grain embargoes or micro economics until I was blue in the face, but if someone told them that farmers were failing due to a Jewish banker conspiracy, that was something that made sense to them. Of all the strange people I've met in my life, none have impacted me more and made less sense to me than people who believe that the color of their skin entitled them to something special from life.

I didn't know how I could fight them, but I knew I had to. Ultimately that fight changed the entire course of my life, but that is another story.

THE GIMP

I spent several years helping the homeless in my spare time. I didn't let myself really feel their pain though. I was always the tender hearted one in the family, and I could worry myself silly about the most minor things. My very first school report card from kindergarten said that I was a very bright child, but tended to worry about things I shouldn't. She really had me pegged. I survived working around hurting people by putting a wall up and not allowing myself to feel their pain. It reminded me of the time I spent working in the morgue in high school. I didn't view the deceased as real. I think I pictured them as plastic mannequins in order to keep my sanity.

I met lots of people who never imagined themselves in a homeless shelter. Lots of people live paycheck to paycheck without stopping to think what they would do if they lost that paycheck. The addicts and the alcoholics are a constant population for those who work in homeless shelters. There are some who find sobriety, but there is always another lost soul in the wings to take their place. It wasn't until the AIDS epidemic started that I began to see people at the shelter who weren't from the edge of the economy. They had been professionals, executives even, but had lost everything when they became ill.

It was the first time in my life that I put any thought into what I would do if I got sick like that. I had always been healthy except for athletic injuries. I'd had several of those, leading to an ankle reconstruction and some serious knee surgeries. I had my bell rung big time at summer camp after falling off a boxcar I shouldn't have been climbing on top of in the first place. There are lots of gimpy former high school athletes in Oklahoma. I guess I thought I was invincible as most young people do. Then a seemingly normal day turned into That Day, the day that everything changed.

By the time that day ended, I had been stabbed and cut a dozen times. I had a torn up knee, a dislocated shoulder, a traumatic brain injury, and a torn up back and neck. The life I had planned was over. The brain that I had always counted on to get me through any problem, was permanently damaged. At first, I actually tried to pretend that I was fine. I became afraid to answer the phone at work for fear someone would ask me a question I couldn't answer. I was afraid to enter a courtroom for the first time. I was afraid to do pretty much anything.

A few months later, I dropped a pack of index cards in court that I had begun to use to try to keep my witness questions in order. It became quickly apparent that I was lost, and the judge called an adjournment. I was requested to withdraw, and I reluctantly agreed. I remember having a large fight with my personal physician. I couldn't understand why people in wheelchairs could still practice law, but I couldn't. She finally got me to understand that someone with a physical disability could still use their brain. My brain was damaged. I was not going to be able to use it the same way I had before.

My doctor arranged for me to have a bunch of neurological tests. I had lost 20 IQ points. I had partial aphasia, which meant I could still understand everything I read, but only partially what I heard. I had lost my ability to understand spoken French and Spanish, and my brain would transpose words I heard. Everything became magnified when I was tired. I became easily agitated. I couldn't concentrate. If I was interrupted in a task, it was very difficult for me to find my place again. I developed a ringing in my ear and I couldn't stand bright lights or loud noises. I had trouble going to sleep, and staying asleep. My memory was like a piece of Swiss cheese. I had trouble learning new things unless it was something I could "peg" onto something I already had in my memory.

The worst part of it all was I developed PTSD, Post Traumatic Stress Disorder. I had officially become a screwball myself. I began to hear things, mostly screaming. I began to see things. Out of nowhere, I would see a hand coming towards my face. In the beginning I thought I was developing hallucinations from something like schizophrenia. Eventually, the doctor realized that I was experiencing flashbacks to my injury. The screaming I was hearing in my head, was my own. There wasn't any real treatment for PTSD at the time. My doctor placed me with group therapy for women with PTSD. It was full of rape survivors and plane crash survivors. There was even a woman who had been tortured in Rwanda. I didn't feel worthy of being with them.

By the time a year had passed, it was apparent that I would not be able to support myself as an attorney. I was able to do small things such as helping people with their wills, or sending nasty notes to insurance companies for widows. I could still do paperwork, but I couldn't talk on the phone. I couldn't do mediations. I couldn't do any work in court. I no longer had any fight left. Most of the time, I couldn't even ask those I was helping for payment. The disability rights attorney would now file for disability benefits for herself. When I entered the examiner's office by myself, she thought my client was running late. When I handed her the forms with my name on them, she was speechless. So was I. I must have done a good job filling them out because I received my own benefits quicker than I had ever successfully received them for a client. Perhaps the ladies in the disability office felt sorry for me and expedited them.

One of the few things I could do was putter around at church. For whatever reason, I never had flashbacks in church. I had volunteered for several years in the Marriage Tribunal, and now I had lots of time to volunteer. I still helped people do disability paperwork. A few months into my forced retirement, a friend from church came to me for support. Her son had died of AIDS recently. She knew of my work with AIDS patients, and so felt like I wouldn't turn her away. Her son had a 5 year old little girl. The girl's mother had been dating a man who had been arrested for molesting my friend's granddaughter. Her mother couldn't handle the court ordered appearances and doctor visits, so she had dumped the girl on my friend's doorstep and skipped the state.

I helped her file for temporary guardianship, and helped her navigate the system. I sat next to her in court every day. I hadn't dealt with that many criminal cases in my career. I did an occasional DUI pleading for one of my clients, but that was an entirely different magnitude of criminal case. My dad had come from a family of New York City policemen. I grew up watching crime shows with him, and reading mystery novels. What you actually see in criminal court is entirely different. It's actually quite long and tedious. That's the main reason I didn't go into criminal law. I had a taste of it in law school and realized I would find it boring.

During this court case, as the accused was testifying, I heard him say something off hand that stuck in my head. When he was being cross-examined about the doctor's report about the little girl, he said loudly that he hadn't done the damage to her the doctor found. Then he said softly that someone else must have gotten to her first. It stuck in my head because there is a line exactly like that in the movie, *In Harm's Way*. At the end of the day, I mentioned it to the prosecutor and the detective. Neither had heard him say it, and neither had the time to review the trial transcript before the next morning in court. She gave me permission to review the transcript to see if the court reporter heard it. The transcript for that day was 100 pages long. There were all sorts of pleadings and evidence reports to wade through to find the actual testimony. I was up most of the night, but finally found what I was looking for. The court reporter had heard it too, and the prosecutor was able to use his words against him during her summation, and he was convicted.

A few weeks later, I was introduced to a priest who was visiting the arch-diocese. I had been at the Pastoral Center to help sort through some annulment files. He worked for a national pro-life charity, which mainly did work around abortion and euthanasia issues, but had a small department that worked on death penalty cases. He asked me if I had ever seen a trial transcript. I told him the story about recently staying up all night to read one. The next thing I knew, I was reviewing trial transcripts for death penalty appeals. I found it was something I could do because it was all in writing. It gave me a purpose, and for the first time since I had been hurt, I felt useful again.

THE BLACK HOLE

My previous experience with a trial transcript had not prepared me for the enormous undertaking I was next to encounter. There is very little money available to defendants for their appeal. In an appeal, you have to find something that happened during the trial that was an error of law. On TV, there is new evidence or a surprise witness. In the real world, if the evidence was discoverable, and you didn't present it at trial, you can't bring it up on appeal. Having an attorney with too much time on her hands, and that you don't have to pay, is a charity's dream.

The courier brought in boxes and boxes of transcripts, evidence forms, depositions, police reports, witness statements, and copies of crime scene photographs. All of which I had to sign for. My roommate came in, and she wasn't able to see over the large file boxes stacked by the door. She was afraid I had decided to move out, and had packed all my things in boxes. When she made it through the maze of boxes, she was rewarded by a coffee table full of quite graphic crime scene photos.

At first, I wasn't sure what I was looking for. I just read page after page, and I was shocked at how inept the defendant's attorney was. He rarely objected to anything. Once the judge actually asked him if he wanted to object to something that was clearly not allowed, and his attorney said no. Although I had no real doubt that the defendant was guilty, I also did not believe that he received a fair trial. By the time I had identified a dozen very substantial issues on appeals, I was also greatly conflicted about what I was doing. I was raised in a culture of hanging judges and the belief in the death penalty. However, I had been an attorney long enough to know that the death penalty was unfairly borne by the poor, the disenfranchised, the mentally ill, the mentally disabled, and by minorities. Still, I couldn't stomach the idea of turning a killer loose back into society.

I called the priest that had talked me into helping with this appeal, and voiced my concerns. He reminded me that if you are truly against abortion, you have to be against it even in cases of rape. If you are truly against euthanasia, you have to be against it for even those in agony. If you are truly against the death penalty, you have to be against it for even the Ted Bundy's and Charles Manson's of the world. There are lots of attorneys to fight for the innocent on death row, but few for the truly guilty. He arranged for me to meet this man on death row.

I had been to this town many times in the past, and I never really gave the prison much thought before. In the past when I saw the signs by the side of the road warning that hitchhikers might be escapees, I chuckled. This time it wasn't funny. The big house certainly lives up to its reputation. It was overwhelming, seemingly nothing but concrete and razor wire. It looked a bit like a concrete bunker from a World War II movie. I wasn't allowed to bring anything inside with me. The steel doors reminded me of the sound bank vault doors make. I was given an escort, a female guard who looked like she could have played professional football. I entered a room that very much looked like something off a cop show. I sat down on a small stool facing a thick sheet of glass with a little telephone receiver on the wall. The first thing that really struck me was the smell. It was a strange combination of hospital cleaner and fear sweat.

Eventually a door opened behind the glass, and a small man walked in and sat down. He told me about his case. He confirmed that he had committed the act he was accused of. He had been high on methamphetamine and only remembers it like it was a dream. He seemed genuinely sorry for what he had done. He told me horrific tales of his childhood, how it led him to start taking drugs in order to numb himself to his life. I asked him what he would do if I helped get his case overturned. He said that his life wouldn't change much because he was serving concurrent sentences for drug offences. I was actually very relieved to hear that. He would be allowed to be placed in another cell block where he could occasionally see the sun and breathe fresh air. He said that he was afraid to go back on the street because he knew he'd start using drugs again, and might hurt someone else.

As we talked, more inmates and visitors came in and out. Some were talking quietly, some ended up crying. I talked to some of the women as they sat waiting for their inmates to come in for their visit. All seemed very likeable. Each asked me if I was his girlfriend. When I explained that I was an attorney, I got inundated with questions and requests for help. As I was leaving, I had a conversation with a woman from England. She had fallen in love with a man on death row after becoming his pen pal. She had recently moved to the US so that she could visit him regularly. She seemed quite sane, but something about her story kind of freaked me out. I was really glad to get outside the walls and breathe clean air again. Several of the women I had met inside asked me to dinner at the rooming house they all seemed to live in.

It was a surreal evening. I was surrounded by a variety of moms, daughters and girlfriends of death row inmates. Some were just spending the night after a day visiting a relative, but many were permanent tenants. I expected them to try to convince me that their men were innocent. Some didn't, but none believed their inmates had received a fair trial. Their men were all addicts, alcoholics, mentally ill or mentally retarded. The broken lives and horror stories I heard could have filled ten seasons of the Dr. Phil show. They had all been thrown away by society long before they committed their crimes. Now they were in the ultimate trash can, clinging until the state took out the garbage.

The moms and daughters I understood. I could imagine quite well if my dad or one of my brothers was here, coming to visit and fight for them. Their stories were also very sad. The other women though, I found fascinating. These were seemingly ordinary women who, for whatever reason, had fallen in love with inmates on death row. It would be easy to say that they were mentally ill themselves in some way, but they weren't. Some were kind of romantic and idealistic. They saw themselves as Princess Charming, who were trying to rescue their princes. Some were bright, professional women who didn't seem to be particularly needy or strange. I suppose that having their boyfriends on death row meant they couldn't play around with other women. Although I did hear the proprietor of the rooming house talk about what happens when two women stay there, who are here to visit the same inmate at the same time.

A couple of these women had married their inmates. I'm not sure what kind of paperwork you'd have to go through to get that approved, and I knew that conjugal visits weren't allowed, but they'd managed it some-how. All of them lived on one hope; that somehow their inmates would be taken off death row, and they would somehow be able to live together, happily ever after. The hardest one's to deal with were the ones still con-vinced that their men were innocent. They spent all their free time and money on attorneys or private detectives.

It was late when I was finally able to excuse myself and make the long drive home. I spent the next several weeks finishing up my review of his death penalty appeal. The attorney who would actually handle the appeal was impressed with the work I'd done. It made me feel really good to think that I could still do some real legal work. Several months later, I got the news that his appeal had been successful. He was offered a new trial, and opted to plead guilty in return for a life sentence instead of facing the death penalty again. He went on to get his high school diploma, and spent his last years teaching other inmates to read. He eventually died of a heart attack. The years of drug use had done their damage, but he had died clean and sober, and was never released to hurt anyone again.

I was eventually able to help 8 men get off death row in 3 different states. None were released from jail; that was my only stipulation. I'd help them get off death row only if they had other charges that would keep them in jail. I just couldn't bring myself to help someone get released to hurt anyone else. I was unsuccessful many more times than successful though. Sometimes the ticking of the clock towards their deaths was as real for me as it was for them. Sometimes I would just know that it was going to happen. Some of the men couldn't really accept the idea until they were strapped on their gurneys. I suppose that was merciful in a way.

I got hate mail sometimes from the family members of the victims. I answered every letter, explaining why I did what I did. After my nephew's murder, I did understand how they felt. I also knew that my nephew could just have easily been on the other side of the knife that night. I might have been one of those women visiting him, waiting for him to die. A few years in, I got a request to stand witness at an execution. Prisoners are allowed to have friends or family present, but this man had neither. I agreed without really thinking through what it would mean to me. As the day came closer, I began to panic a bit. I talked it over with my priest, and there wasn't anything sinful about attending an execution so long as I wasn't the one conducting it. I had never wanted to get a stay of execution for anyone as much as I wanted this one.

The day came. Although I had been to visit this death row many times, I had never been to the facility where the death chamber was. The waiting area was separate for the friends and family of the victim. I was by myself. We were called, and filed in. I was last. Present were policemen and prosecutors who were involved in the original investigation, in addition to the prison guards. There were a couple of reporters as well, but no cameras. The room faced a large window with curtains. It was rather hot, and we all fell into an uncomfortable silence.

The curtains opened, and my client walked in and sat down on a bed that had two table extensions by the arms. He looked over and saw me, and smiled a little. He stared at the ceiling while they strapped him down, one guard per limb. The curtains closed. A man next to me asked angrily if I was here for "that piece of filth." I quietly said that I was one of his representatives. He asked me how I could work for rapists and murderers. I explained that I was opposed to the death penalty. He said that this was the only way he was going to get closure for the death of his sister. All I could say was that I truly hoped he did get closure and could find some healing.

Just then, the curtains re-opened. My client had been hooked up to some tubing, and his lower half was covered by a sheet. There was a chaplain standing by his lower legs, and another man next to his head. The man standing next to him asked if he had any last words. He looked around, and quietly said he was sorry. He looked at me, and looked at the ceiling. The man next to him took off his glasses and nodded towards a small window. My client started to breathe deeply as if he was starting to hyperventilate. He opened his eyes and looked around. His face looked terrified. His body started to shake and he began to loudly gasp for air. I looked around behind me at the guards, wondering if this was normal. I could tell by the looks on their faces that it wasn't.

He gasped and shuddered, for what seemed like for hours. A medical technician entered the room with a look of panic on his face. Someone in the gallery began to throw up. One of the guards behind me passed out, and fell across several witnesses, knocking everyone in his path to the ground. The curtains were pulled closed again as someone else began to vomit. I felt light headed, and put my head between my knees. Several more guards came in and ushered the other witnesses out. I was escorted into an office and asked to wait until someone came to talk to me. About 45 minutes later, a very flustered man came in and explained that my client had been officially declared dead. I asked what had happened, and he wouldn't answer. He said there would be information at a later time.

I left the building and sat in my car for quite a while before I felt able to drive. I'm not sure how I got home. I got a call the next day from the priest who originally recruited me to do this work. He wanted me to speak publicly about what I had seen. He thought it would help publicize some of the issues with the death penalty. I declined. My former client, no matter what he had done, was still entitled to his human dignity. Talking about how awful his death was publicly, especially for publicity purposes, wasn't dignified. His crime had been the worst one of all the cases I'd dealt with. He had assaulted a woman while high on a number of illegal drugs. He killed her to leave no witnesses. He was so high that he did a number of mutilations to the body, trying to figure out if she was really dead. His accomplice got life. He got death.

He was the last death penalty client I dealt with. My heart wasn't in it anymore. I felt dirty, maybe even violated. My soul ached at how much evil there was in the world. I suppose I was just burned out. I found my-self thinking about my great-grandfather. He'd been a NYPD detective in the late 1800's. My dad told me once about how his grandfather told him that in his day rapists never made it to the police station. They tended to have accidents. I certainly don't agree with that idea, but understood why it happened. I wonder to this day, if we still did public executions and if what I had seen was a spectator sport, how long we would still allow the death penalty. We tell ourselves that we give murderers too many appeals. They get to live too long. They have easier deaths than their victims did. We have washed our hands of it and made it seem like we are just putting someone to sleep, like a dying cat. I don't actually think we have tried to make executions easier for the benefit of the murderers. We have done it to make it easier on ourselves.

I also thought about the dead girl and her family. I wonder if her brother did get closure; I doubt it. I have had lots of contact with victims' families over the years. The few people I met who had truly begun to heal from a tragedy were those who gave forgiveness. They didn't wait until the perpetrator was convicted or executed. If you put off the grieving or healing process for years, waiting for appeals to be upheld and an execution to occur, you get stuck. Your whole world is about seeing someone punished for your loved one's death. When that person is dead, so is your purpose for living. I decided that I had spent enough time with the dead, and wanted to rejoin the living.

ARLENE

During the years I volunteered with the homeless, the mentally ill, and those on death row, I had a roommate. She came to live with me before I got hurt. As a child, I was always bringing home strays; turtles, dogs, pretty much anything but cats. This was a habit that was hard to break, even as an adult. One of the therapists who helped with breakout sessions at workshops came to me about a woman she worked with. Arlene had been living at a halfway house after being diagnosed with bipolar disorder. She had been severely injured at work, and after having neck surgery, she had a breakdown. While she was in the hospital getting stabilized on medication, her husband moved in with her best friend, leaving her homeless on top of everything else. The halfway house was a bad fit for her because she hadn't recovered from her neck surgery, and wasn't capable of doing the chores the halfway house required.

She needed a place to stay to finish her recuperation. She had no money because her company disability plan had not kicked in yet. She couldn't go to a homeless shelter because they required people to leave during the day. She couldn't sleep on a mat on the floor anyway. So she came home with me, still in a neck brace. She was an ultra-rapid cycling bipolar, which meant she could go from mania to depression several times a week. She was also a recovering alcoholic, which was not unusual for people with bipolar disorder. They often self-medicated with alcohol.

It was okay at first, but after she had lived with me for a few weeks, she became a bit chaotic. She slashed her wrists several times; not deep enough to need stitches, but deep enough to spread blood everywhere. I found myself once more unsure of what I was going to find when I came home. Sometimes she would disappear for several days at a time. I had no idea where she was going. Eventually she told me that she was going to visit her sons. She had a 3 year old living with her mother in Arkansas and an infant living with her ex-husband. The older boy had a different father, so when she went to the hospital, her ex only took the baby. It also explained why he was so quick to move in with another woman, so that she could take care of the baby. Apparently her breakdown started as a bad case of post-partum depression

At that time I did a lot of traveling for my job, where I would go out to meet farmers or performing mediations for them with their creditors. I found it easier to just take Arlene with me, rather than be afraid of finding a mess when I got home. She seemed to become more stable from this, and she began to open up to me to about her past. She had been the victim of childhood sexual abuse and a lot of physical abuse. Being alone gave her too much time to think about things she didn't want to. She began coming with me to work, to the courthouse, and on out of town trips. It seemed very strange at the time. My secretary understood what I was doing, but the rest of the office staff didn't. There started to be whispers. I've never really cared what other people thought about me, and her mental illness issues were her private business. My secretary knew because she was the only one who needed to know. It was a bit like having a shadow.

One of my trips took us close to the Arkansas border, so I thought it might be nice for me to make a weekend of it and allow Arlene to visit with her son. The entire trip was quite surreal. By this time, I had learned that one of Arlene's childhood abusers was her father. His family was a stereotypically hillbilly family. They were barely literate, had boundary and abuse issues, and were generally a scary bunch. Her son, John, was being raised like some kind of feral animal. He spent all day in just underwear and snow boots. He ran around kicking things and watching TV. He mostly just ate ice cream. What shocked me the most is that no one in her family seemed to be able to understand that he wasn't normal.

The last night we were there, I almost called the police. I discovered that Arlene's mom had been bathing John with her. I thought she had just been bathing him, but when I saw her come out of the bathroom in her robe with wet hair, I was told that she felt it was easier to just put him in the bathtub while she was taking her own bath. As an attorney, I was a mandatory reporter in Oklahoma, but we were in Arkansas. I also knew that if I filed a complaint, John would be placed in foster care because his mother was not capable of taking care of him, and his father had never been in his life. I decided to get more information first.

I spent several sleepless nights after that weighing my options. I decided to discuss it with my pastor. He agreed that I couldn't leave John with his grandparents. I felt that there was only one solution I could live with. I agreed to take custody of John, and he came to live with us. This began a long period of taking John to doctors to try to diagnose his apparent disabilities. At the time Arlene discovered she was pregnant with him, she was working at a printing company. As part of her duties, she routinely used benzene to clean the presses. Exposure to that can lead to a lot of birth defects. It was so serious that Arlene had considered having an abortion. She couldn't bring herself to terminate the pregnancy, and he seemed to be born fine. The defects weren't visible on the surface.

It became apparent very quickly that he had no socialization skills. His idea of playing with other children was to stand across the street and scream until the other children turned to look at him, and then he ran away. He was showing all the prodromal symptoms that those who later develop schizophrenia have. He couldn't understand normal body language. If someone on the playground got up in his face in an aggressive way, he would misunderstand. He thought that the boy wanted to be that close to him, that it meant he wanted to be friends. When the boy pushed or hit him, John would get his feelings hurt because he couldn't understand why someone who wanted to be friends would hit him.

We signed him up to work with a therapist who did play therapy. We actually had to teach him how to play and how to read body language. He was capable of understanding it to a certain extent, but always had trouble making friends or understanding other kids. We tried a variety of outside activities like baseball and soccer, but the only thing that he truly engaged with was the Boy Scouts. In little league, it took him two years to get his first hit. When he got on base by a walk or hit by a pitch, I had to stand at the fence closest to first base so that I could yell at him when it was time to run. Otherwise, he would just stand at the base until the next runner literally ran into him. He had lots of fun though. Just being with other kids and sitting on the bench cheering, made him very happy. Never getting to play would normally bother a player and their parents, but John was satisfied to just be included.

Arlene had good days and bad. At least once every 6 months she had to be placed in the hospital to re-stabilize on her medication. Sometimes she would go off her medication without me knowing it until she was in crisis. There were several more suicide attempts. Once she attempted to jump out of the car on the highway. Another time she jumped in front of a city bus right in the view of her son. She had to be hospitalized several times a year for overdoses. Unfortunately, the injuries that she received on the job had left her in constant pain.

There were times she went to multiple doctors to double or triple dip on pain medicine. Other times she underwent bizarre treatments. Once she had a gel injected into her knee. Another time, she had an X-ray treatment designed to burn away nerves on her spine. She repeatedly had injections in various parts of her body for temporary relief. One of her doctors disappeared before being arrested for drug offences. She traded and bartered pain medicine back and forth with other addicts. I also dealt with constant pain from my injuries, but watching Arlene and her friends go around in circles with narcotics, I was never tempted to use them for my own pain.

During her manic phases, she often self-medicated with alcohol. She was a different person under the influence of alcohol. Sometimes she was a happy drunk, likely to walk into a neighborhood bar and buy a round for the house. I discovered these splurges as multiple hundreds of dollars charges on my credit card. Sometimes she would disappear for days at a time when on a bender. She borrowed my car once to go to a doctor's appointment. When she didn't return in time to pick me up after work, I caught a ride home with my secretary.

Her son was waiting in the yard in the dark. He'd been alone for several hours after coming home from kindergarten. I spent the next several hours calling hospitals and police stations trying to find her. Finally in the middle of the night, I got a call from a neighboring county jail. She had taken the police on a high speed chase in my car before crashing it. It took six Oklahoma highway patrolmen to take her into custody. Then she kicked out the patrol car's dashboard and radio. It took a lot of money to repair my car and keep her out of jail. It might have been better for her in the long run to have spent some time in jail. I did everything I could to keep her out of jail, not for her, but for her son. I was afraid that having his mom in jail would have done damage to him. I was also afraid he'd end up in foster care. Through it all, I cleaned up one mess after another, trying to shield John from the worst part of his childhood.

She would have long periods of time where she was fairly stable, and sometimes these periods would last months at a time. These respites were heavenly. Each time, I prayed that she had turned some kind of corner and the old Arlene was gone. During one of these remissions, she obtained custody of her younger son. Now I was responsible for two children in addition to their mother. One day I saw myself in the mirror and didn't recognize my reflection; being a caretaker was wearing on me. I was taking care of everyone but myself. I'd become angry and self-destructive. Worst of all, I had no idea how to get out of the mess I'd found myself in.

Somehow I held myself together, but it came at a cost. I spent my time going between doctor's appointments with Arlene during the day, and spending every night and weekend at the little league field or Boy Scout meeting. I was a nurse and a cook and a chauffeur, but I was no longer me. For the first time I realized what the families of my clients had gone through. I had known caretakers before. The family from church who had a mentally retarded son, the family friend who had a sick mom who lived on a hospital bed in their living room, my own grandmother who took care of my grandfather when he developed dementia, they were all caretakers. I understood now the feeling of never having a day off. I understood feeling like I was being suffocated.

Eventually, I couldn't take it anymore. My body rebelled. My blood pressure shot up so high that I had an angina attack. I thought it was a heart attack, and that I was going to die. When I was released from the hospital, I was determined to start taking back my life. I had floated along with the current for so long that I knew standing up to the current was going to cause some ripples. Arlene fought back by getting sicker. She started having more frequent episodes. These were some of the first real episodes she'd had since her younger son had come to live with us. She started to drink again. She started having paranoid episodes. I stopped rescuing her and made her experience her own consequences for the first time in over a decade.

This meant her boys started to see her in a different light. I no longer attempted to shield them from the worst of her behavior. I hadn't planned this, but it was an unfortunate side effect of my starting to care about myself first. I was no longer willing to put all my time and money into the younger boy's baseball teams. He had been used to getting everything he wanted, and was well trained in the art of playing his divorced parents off of each other. He had been so shielded that when his mother acted out, he blamed me rather than her. I guess that was the only way he could endure her increasingly out of control behavior. In one terrifying episode, the police had responded by taking Arlene in for a 72 hour hold to get her back on her medication. In fighting with the police, she almost got the officer's gun away from him. After she was safely removed from our apartment, I had to serve the officer some coffee and allow him to calm down. He said that being shot by his own weapon was a constant fear.

The boys were both very upset by the episode. The older boy dealt with it by convincing himself that it never happened. The younger boy convinced himself that I had been abusive and that's why his mom tried to grab a gun. He began to imagine me capable of many horrors. In a relatively short time, he returned to his dad's custody, never to return. The older boy had nowhere else to go. Fortunately, he was just 6 months from graduating from high school. I encouraged him to go into the military; it was the best way I could think of to get him away from his mother. I told him that as soon as he turned 18, he would be his mother's next of kin, and the calls from the hospitals and jails would start coming to him rather than me. He understood what that would mean, and left just before his 18th birthday.

I repeatedly explained to Arlene that I intended to restart my life. I told her I wasn't going to sign a new lease when our present one expired, and that she needed to be making some plans for herself. I began going to the gym, I entered therapy, and began training to do missionary work. My head injury was not going to allow me to practice law again, but I felt like I could still be productive. I hadn't been able to travel for several years, so I was very excited at the idea of going somewhere new. I was going to be training women to sew, so that they might get a job in a factory rather than selling their bodies in the sex trade. Instead of preparing herself for a time when I would be leaving, Arlene started acting out in ways she hadn't since the time she first came to live with me. Those behaviors which had convinced me to allow her to stay 15 years previously were now reaffirming to me that I needed to move on. The difference was that I no longer had a small child to worry about.

Arlene seemed to think that if she was sick enough, I would stay. When I got calls from the hospital, I no longer got upset. In the past I would sit next to her bed, praying for her to get well. When out of control, she would pull out IV's, fight against the orderlies, scream and threaten. Before, I would be afraid; I would be afraid she was going to hurt me or one of the boys. I was afraid she would disappear with the boys and something would happen to them. Somehow, I got over my fear. I'm sure a lot of it was due to me no longer being afraid for the boys because they were both gone. I also think that I finally realized that there was nothing more she could do to harm me that I had not done to myself in the last 15 years. Ultimately though, I began to be able to separate her from her illness. When she was sober and sane, she was a caring, intelligent person. When her diseases got the better of her, I began to be able to tell myself that I was not mad at her, but at her disease.

Still, she couldn't understand that I was preparing to leave. I think she believed that if she didn't accept it, it wouldn't happen. I spent weeks at a time away on retreat or in classes preparing myself to become a missionary. Every time I left town, she put herself into crisis. It reminded me of her first months with me. I took classes at night, and she would have a crisis every week on that day until I eventually had to drop the class. This time, I did not allow her behavior to force me to quit. If she cut herself, she had to get herself to the doctor or emergency room. I didn't drop everything to rescue her. I was in a place where I couldn't easily use a telephone. This infuriated her because she could not reach me immediately. Sometimes my only contact for weeks was email, which she had trouble using. Finally she had an epiphany. She entered the hospital to have her knee replaced. After she was taken to the operating room, I left and went to the gym for a water aerobics class. She woke up and I wasn't there. I wasn't trying to be unkind. I was trying to prepare her, and take care of myself first.

When I came to the hospital later to visit, she was livid. She informed me that the doctor had destroyed her knee because I hadn't been there in the waiting room. She tried to convince me that he had come out of the operating room to ask her "medical advocate" which direction he should take in the surgery. She was convinced that had I been there, I would have directed him to do the surgery a different way. No amount of explaining that had the doctor asked my opinion, I would have told him to use his best judgment, which is what he had done in any case, and that therefore my not being in the waiting room had made no difference. I grew tired of listening to her yell at me, so I left, and didn't return to visit. I spoke to her on the phone each day. She seemed to be descending into psychosis. I had tried so hard over the years to help her, but finally realized that she was either beyond my help or just didn't want help.

The next big shock came when she was released from the hospital. She assumed that she would be returning home for me to take care of her as

I had dozens of times over the years after her hospitalizations. Instead I had arranged with her doctor to have her taken to the rehabilitation hospital to begin her recuperation. I talked to her each day, but did not visit, and only came when she was able to take care of herself enough to return to our apartment. She returned home full of anger and expected to be able to unleash her bile on me, but I left almost immediately for the last time. Except for the few possessions I was taking with me, especially my sewing machines, everything else I owned had been put in storage. It was physical, visual evidence to her that I was truly leaving. She became violent, and I truly felt in danger. I do wonder what she did after she saw me leaving in the airport shuttle.

I was as far away as possible, yet she seemed incapable of letting go. She sent horrific emails. She must have spent hundreds of dollars in phone charges calling to scream at me thousands of miles away. She called my friends and family back home telling them bizarre things about me. She told our landlady that I had left her in the lurch, unable to pay her rent. I had paid all my rent in full before leaving so the landlady told her that wasn't true. She told her mother that I had been put in jail for abusing her sons. She told my mother that I was on the run from debt collectors. She told my friends that I was an embezzler. Over a year later when I had settled in Canada, she called my future husband at 4am to tell him that I was wanted by the FBI for bank fraud. She threatened to come to Canada to kill me. At least I knew that was an empty threat. Her criminal record would keep her from being able to cross the border.

Other times she would call completely sane, and I tried to stay in contact with her. We had lived together for over 15 years. I liked hearing how she was doing, and what the boys were up to. I sent her little care packages with tea from Chinatown. I was glad to hear that she had made the decision to move back to Arkansas to be close to her parents. I thought that they might be able to help her stabilize finally. I had worried that maybe I was the reason she never got well. If I hadn't been doing things for her, then she might have been forced sooner to stay on her meds and stay clean and sober. I always encouraged her to stay straight, but cleaning up her messes meant she never had real consequences for her behavior.

At first she seemed to do fine in Arkansas. She was placed in a government housing project that was geared for the disabled. It seemed to be a safe environment. About a year after she moved in there, she seemed to start to unravel. She had been caught digging up the flower beds around the apartments. Sometimes she told me she had been looking for diamonds, and other times dinosaur fossils. Eventually she was asked to leave. From that point forward our conversations were fewer and stranger. She told me she had moved in with a woman, but didn't know her name. She called me to complain that people had been breaking in and stealing her medication. Her calls were frightening, but there was nothing I could do 3000 miles away. I kept hoping her parents would step in, but she had broken off communication with them.

The last time I talked to her was right after my first book was published. She had seen it advertised for sale on the website of a large US department store. It infuriated her. I'm not sure what upset her most, the possibility that I had said something about her in the book, or that I was having a good life. She mostly screamed obscenities at me and hung up. I never got to talk to her again. I tried calling the number several times, but there was no answer. I sent letters, but got no response. I even sent a note to her parents asking if she was okay, but they never responded. I hoped that she had been placed into some kind of treatment facility or group home.

A few months later I reconnected with her oldest son on Facebook. He told me his mom had died about a month after I last spoke with her. She had gotten sick and didn't immediately go to the doctor, but finally ended up sick enough that she went to the hospital. With her history of hospitalizations and drug seeking behavior, she was often made to wait long periods of time in emergency rooms. I always had to advocate for her to be seen. By the time they got around to treating her, the pneumonia that she had come in with was too advanced to treat in time to save her. She had contracted the H1N1 flu. With her history of asthma, smoking, and lung issues, she needed to be treated quickly when she came down with something. I still feel guilty that I wasn't there to take her to the doctor immediately, or force her into the hospital. 57 is too young to die.

She had lived such a hard life and her body had been through so much that I know she is more comfortable now, but kids don't stop needing their moms when they turn 18. I still wonder if she died of bird flu or of her mental illness. Without one, would she have died of the other?

The one thing my 20 year relationship with Arlene taught me is that no matter how much I wanted someone to get better, I had no real control. First, the person needed to want to get better. They needed help to accept the idea that they had an illness, and that they would need to accept the idea that they would have to take medication for the rest of their lives. They also had to deal with any other issues that their mental illness had caused. Sometimes their family of origin was so unhealthy, that it led to their illness. Sometimes the illness had taken so long to be diagnosed that it had destroyed the person's relationships with their friends and family. In Arlene's case, her abuse as a child had certainly contributed to her illness and addiction issues. Self-medicating with street drugs and alcohol not only made her illness worse, it led to addictions that complicated her treatment. Even worse, growing up in a culture where everyone is expected to be self-reliant, she got no help from her family. They were ashamed of her. They were ashamed of her illness. Maybe they were just burned out from her.

I sometimes wonder at night when I can't sleep, if there was something, anything, I could have done differently. The answer I always get is that to keep her alive, I would have had to give up the rest of my life to taking care of her, and it still might not have been enough. I just couldn't do it anymore than I could have saved my nephew, David, from his addictions. You can help them get better only if they are willing and capable of doing the hard work it requires.

VOICES AGAIN

When I was preparing to go overseas to do mission work, I was encouraged to get pen pals. Most people in the program had friends and family to keep in touch with, but living with Arlene all those years made me realize it had cost me both. Any friends I had or might have had were run off by Arlene. She was difficult to be around. I found out later from the nun who ran the missionary training that every time she called to talk to me when I wasn't home, Arlene said horrible things about me. I contacted old friends who had stopped communicating with me, and found out that she had done the same to them. She had isolated me, and I had never really noticed it. I think one of the reasons she hated me going to the swimming pool was that she couldn't follow me there. She tried coming to my water aerobics class a couple of times, but it set off her asthma. Making friends in the pool was like making friends for the first time on the playground when I was a child.

I joined a website for Catholics, and started making lots of friends there, even if they were just electronic. At least I could communicate with them while on the other side of the planet. I began corresponding with a man named Austin, who lived in Alberta in Canada. As a typical American, I didn't really know that much about Canada. I had this vague notion of something north of New York because there was a baseball team there, and I knew there was something north of Washington State called British Columbia. When he told me he lived north of Montana, I said that no one could live north of Montana except Eskimos. Luckily he was a trained geographer and was able to set me straight.

As time went by, he told me lots about himself. I had a lot of time during the day to write long emails to all my new friends. He had trained in geography, but had a variety of specialities which took him all over the world, including spending 3 months in a tent at the South Pole looking for meteorites. He sent me a photo of him giving Pope John Paul II the small Papal flag he took with him to Antarctica. He returned with frostbite damage to the nerves in his feet and hands and damaged lungs. After that he had collaborated with his father on some very strange research projects and publications. One of his specialities was in "discovering" ancient comets. His father, who was a retired medieval scholar and spoke several dead languages, would translate ancient Norse or Celtic sagas that included accounts of comets. Austin would then take those sightings and establish which comet those scribes were de-scribing. He is one of the few Fellows of the International Academy of Astronautics in the field of historical astronomy.

Finally, out of the blue one day, he admitted to me that he had schizo-phrenia. That surprised me. I asked him if he took his medicine, and if he intended to stay on his medicine. The last thing I needed was another friend like Arlene, even one that was thousands of miles away. He told me that he had always taken his meds, never once gone off them, and accepted that he had to take them the rest of his life. I said, okay then, no problem. He thought I didn't know what the word schizophrenia meant. He'd had research partners break off communication in the middle of a project when they found out. He had family members who pretended he didn't exist. I told him I'd had a bad head injury and PTSD, but refused to tell any of my family about it for fear they would be ashamed of me.

As we talked, we discovered that we had been at the same place several times before. He had majored in geography and I had been in forestry. He had gone to school in Texas. We had attended some of the same con-ferences together. We had even been at the same Explorer's Club dinner once. Yet, we had never met. We liked the same books and movies, and we had even become disabled around the same age. I decided to take my leave time and go to meet him in Canada. My missionary supervisor insisted on doing a criminal background check on everyone that I'd be dealing with. There was Austin of course, and the woman from his church, Janet, who had offered me her spare room to stay in during my visit, and also the woman that I would be staying with in Florida while getting ready for my trip. Once back in St. Pete, I dealt with the rest of my possessions that had been in storage, and hopped on a bus to Alberta. I couldn't stand the idea of getting back on an airplane anytime soon.

My bus finally arrived after midnight. Janet had driven Austin to the bus station, but began to get tired of waiting on my overdue bus. She had even begun to think that I was just a figment of his imagination. She told him she was leaving, but had just gone to sit around the corner at the depot. I was exhausted when I got off the bus. He said we'd have to take a taxi just about the time that Janet popped around the corner. He wanted to take me out to eat, but the only place in the neighborhood still open that late was the dinner attached to the Alcoholics Anonymous clubhouse. Janet didn't think that was an appropriate place to take a guest, and went home.

We had a nice turkey dinner. Turns out, it was Canadian Thanksgiving weekend. Afterwards, he walked me to Janet's apartment. She was still awake and kept me up until 4am talking. I've met hardened detectives who couldn't have interrogated me harder than I got that night. I spent the next month or so being interrogated by just about everyone I met. My southern accent made me stand out. People in the neighborhood and at church seemed fascinated by me. I know they weren't trying to be impolite exactly, but everyone was curious about a "normal" woman who wanted to have anything to do with a guy who had schizophrenia.

Explaining that I had lots of experience with the mentally ill didn't seem to help. They assumed that if I had experience with mental cases, I was probably one too. Almost half the people I met asked me if I also had schizophrenia. When I said no, they were shocked. Even funnier is that the people, who didn't ask, naturally assumed that I had schizophrenia. If Austin had been blind or deaf, people wouldn't have automatically assumed that I would also have to be blind or deaf in order to want to go out with him. I was in Canada for a couple of weeks, running around town with Janet, meeting people, taking in the sites, before Austin got up the nerve to try to kiss me. I think my first mistake was cooking for him. I had forgotten about the adage of the way to a man's heart is through his stomach.

AUSTIN

The news that the old maid was going to finally get married, spread like wildfire through my friends and family back home. I don't think my mom knew what to feel. On the one hand, she was afraid for me. She had been married to a man with schizophrenia, and her experiences with him clouded her opinion of Austin for a long time. On the other hand, she was happy I was happy, but unhappy that I was going to be thousands of miles away in a foreign country. I think she wanted to ignore it and hoped that it wouldn't happen.

Austin's family didn't want to ignore our impending wedding; they wanted to put a stop to it. First, someone in his family convinced some governmental officials that I needed to be investigated. Their thinking was that any person who wanted to marry this mentally ill man must have an ulterior motive. I was forced to undergo a second FBI background check, and additional screening by the RCMP and the Canadian Security Intelligence Service, the Canadian version of the CIA. I was being investigated as a potential terrorist. I passed every screening, still the threat loomed over us.

We tried to jump through every hoop requested so that I could stay in the country. We tried to handle the matter discretely, and through proper channels to no avail. Finally, when I was two weeks away from getting deported, Austin called in a favor from a friend. Someone he knew from a provincial schizophrenia organization was a retired CSIS agent. He had to retire when his son came down with the illness, but still had many useful contacts. He made a phone call, and Austin's Member of Parliament made a phone call, and my threat of deportation finally went away.

Not being able to get me kicked out of the country didn't dissuade his family. We decided to quickly marry civilly to make it much harder for his family to try other tactics to get me deported. The next prong of their attack was financial. They must have believed that I was after Austin's money. The fact that I made more money than he did, didn't change their minds that I was a gold digger. We were threatened with homelessness. Austin had purchased his home many years before, but after we married, I discovered that when he purchased it with the help of a family member who was a realtor, the home hadn't been placed in Austin's name even though he had paid the down payment and mortgage.

When Austin realized that he had no legal right to stay in the home he had invested tens of thousands of dollars in, he began to panic. He was worried that something would happen to him and leave me homeless in a foreign country. He even began to have chest pains. His family began to threaten to sell the house out from under him. He requested to sign a lease agreement, or a lease to own agreement. He offered to buy the house all over again with a new mortgage. We sent letters, emails, faxes, and made phone calls, but they refused to speak to him about it. He felt like a failure for having been taken advantage of by someone he loved.

I didn't care about money; I've never really ever cared about it. I know that stress is toxic to someone with Austin's illness. No amount of money is worth him becoming sick. So, we walked away. That was preferable to living with homelessness hanging over our heads. Austin walked away from his $25,000 down payment and 7 years' worth of mortgage payments and upgrades to the house. He had to fight with the bank to get them to stop taking automatic payments out of his bank account for someone else's mortgage. We started over, but we were together, and there was nothing his family could do to make us homeless after that.

Their next assault was on our marriage. We had been forced to marry civilly, but were still waiting to be allowed our church ceremony. 3 days before our wedding was scheduled, we received a call from our priest. Someone from Austin's family had called him, and told him that Austin was off his medicine and beating me. I'm not sure how they could possibly know that he was off his medication. In addition, Austin is on one of the long acting injectable medications. He goes to his doctor's office every two weeks, without fail, to receive it. His doctor would know immediately if he had missed a dose, and so would I, since I went with him for each injection.

More importantly, anyone who knows me knows that had Austin ever gotten out of hand with me, just as soon as he regained consciousness, I would have him hospitalized. I was raised around nothing but boys, all bigger and older than me. I could handle anything Austin might throw at me, and then some. When things go bump in the night, I'm the one who jumps up with the baseball bat. Austin is a bookworm who is a complete gentleman. Unfortunately, our parish priest had the responsibility to investigate his family's concerns, and our wedding was cancelled.

We spent the next 6 months trying to convince him that we were both competent to marry. I had to get letters from my doctor back in Florida that my brain injury did not leave me incompetent. Austin had to supply letters from his doctors that his illness was well controlled by medication. Our priest talked to my friends and family members back home. He wanted to know if I had been married before. He thought that I was just marrying Austin because my biological clock was ticking and I was desperate to have a baby. He had even been told that I was an embezzler on the run.

My youngest brother was a good sport about all the questions; he had to deal with me being in a panic. I suppose he was just grateful his old maid sister wasn't going to come live with him. I think it was hard for our priest to conceptualize a family that would lie to try to stop a wedding. Finally he talked to a retired priest that had known Austin's family for 20 years. Once he explained that this is how Austin's family normally acted, our priest knew he'd been duped. He rescheduled our wedding early on a Sunday morning. He didn't unlock the church, but brought us through the rectory. A couple of my friends that arrived late, stood at the side door and pounded to be let in. He didn't stop the ceremony; all it made him do was talk quicker.

I had been suffering from a chest cold, and had lost my voice. Austin had gotten water in his ears that morning in the shower, and couldn't hear. So, I was whispering, Austin was shouting, and our priest was talking as fast as an auctioneer. All the while, the doors to the church were being pounded on. It was surreal, a bit like getting married in a bombed out basement during the Blitz. I sometimes wonder if he was afraid that Austin's family members might show up with shotguns and pitchforks to stop the service. All in all, it was just as crazy as anything else in our lives.

A year later, his former house was sold, clearing over $200 000 in profit. It made Austin furious all over again that he had been cheated. I thought he was going to have a stroke. He threatened to file a grievance with the real estate board. There were several irregularities in the original purchase of the house. In the face of that pressure, he was given back his down payment, but only if he would sign an agreement to have no further contact with the parties involved. He also had to agree to never speak publicly about being cheated. However, I never agreed to remain silent. I don't think people should be able to hide from their misdeeds. That's especially so when it's someone who has taken advantage of someone else who is vulnerable. Austin had trusted and been betrayed. Having handled estate issues, I've seen many family members turn on each other over money. It's always made me sick to my stomach.

People often view the mentally ill as monsters. I have found the opposite. They spend most of their lives afraid. Either their medication or their illness or a combination of both can make them unable to defend themselves. That's especially true with schizophrenia. That illness robs them of the ability to read body language, to understand hidden agenda, or to catch nuance. Add the sedating effect of the medication, and they can be as helpless as small children when it comes to being taken advantage of. The stereotype is that schizophrenics are dangerous. The truth is that they are by far more likely to be the victim of crimes than the perpetrator.

A sobering statistic is that two thirds of all female schizophrenics have been raped. Of those, half have been more than once. The radar system that we have built in to prevent us from going into a dark alley with a strange man doesn't work right when you have this illness.

The fact is being taken advantage of financially is common for those with mental illnesses. Austin felt humiliated. Nothing I said could make him feel better. Time helped, but every now and then it rears back up. I felt bad too, but not for the same thing. I felt like I had been the catalyst for destroying his relationship with his family. I certainly never saw that coming, and I certainly never wanted that to happen. I tried to assuage my hurt feelings, thinking to myself that his family thought they were protecting Austin. They didn't know me. They thought we were getting married too quickly. I suppose we did, but one thing about long distance relationships is that since we couldn't do things like go to the movies or dinner, we had to talk instead. When you apply for immigration, you have to give proof that your relationship is valid, and not just for the purpose of getting into the country. We were able to print off 400 pages of single space emails, and that didn't include the hours spent text messaging. His family had no way of knowing how much we had gotten to know each other.

At first, they thought I would stay with Austin just long enough to get on his health insurance; my health insurance coverage was actually better in the US. Then, they thought I was just here until I received my permanent residency, and I'd divorce him. That came and went. Then they thought I would stay just long enough for us to pay off our condo and steal it from him. That also didn't happen. Finally, they thought I'd leave when my citizenship was granted. Nope. He actually got a call where one of them asked, "Why is she still here!?!" The idea that a sane woman could want to marry a man with schizophrenia was something they just couldn't accept. As we approach our ten year anniversary, I wonder if they will ever accept or acknowledge that they were wrong about me. I've long since given up on receiving an apology.

One thing I did learn was there was a reason the Gospel of Mark says, "'For this reason a man shall leave his father and mother and be joined to his wife, and the two shall become one flesh.' So they are no longer two but one flesh." When Austin hurt, I hurt. When his family tried to hurt me, it hurt him every bit as much. It reminded me of the mentally ill clients I had. Often their families wanted to treat them as normal and expected them to act that way, or they would try to infantilize them and run their lives for them. It sure felt different from this side of the fence though.

FRAT HOUSE MOM

When I married Austin, it was as if I married all of his unmarried mentally ill friends. I'm told that only 10% of those with schizophrenia are married. He did warn me that he was a very intellectual man, but that everyday tasks eluded him. I knew my work was cut out for me when I found that he had been using his oven to store books. He had books everywhere, and so I had to tame the books and boxes of papers. I discovered over $1 000 worth of loose coins in the house. He lived like a confirmed bachelor.

I think the funniest story was about 6 months after we married. We were having dinner with friends. This couple is older than we are, but have two adult sons with schizophrenia. She had served as my maid of honor since I didn't know anyone when I first arrived in Canada. She made an off-hand comment about how much nicer Austin was dressing since we'd gotten married. She said it was nice to see him in ironed shirts. Austin froze with his fork half way to his mouth and said, "You're ironing my shirts?" We all exploded in laughter. The longer I'm with him, the more he reminds me of my father. He's a very gentle guy, if a bit clueless about ordinary life. He's much more comfortable with a book in his hand than a hammer. He once cut his finger handing me an ordinary set of pliers. We still don't know exactly how. Thankfully his manhood isn't threatened by my handling all the home repairs. I shipped 32 boxes of possessions to Canada. Half of them were tools.

He spent half of his time serving on governmental committees dealing with disability issues, especially for the mentally ill. The other half of the time he gave lectures at the university or speeches to the public. Before I knew it, he had me speaking too. I had always been a good public speaker, but this wasn't something I was used to talking about publicly. When I would tell a joke at Austin's expense, the crowd would gasp. I would have to explain that as a southern woman it is my God-given right to give my husband the dickens. If I don't, then I'm not treating him like a husband or a man. I never wanted to treat him like a child, like someone not competent to handle his own affairs or make his own decisions, and I especially didn't want to treat him like he was my patient and I was his nurse.

Most people with Austin's illness are either too sick to speak publicly, or they do not want to be "outed" in public. Homosexuals may be out of the closet now, but those with serious mental illnesses are still mostly buried deeply in theirs. It's still not easy for him to be this public. He's always afraid that people will see him as some kind of monster and be afraid of him. He also worries that he might have another psychotic break and hurt me without knowing what he is doing. That doesn't worry me. I know that schizophrenics are much more likely to be the victim of a crime than to commit one. Of course when one of them does act out, it is usually something so bizarre that it makes the front page of the newspaper. The one thing those people have in common is that they aren't on proper medication. They have never been properly diagnosed, gone off their medication, or the medication has simply stopped working.

A year after we were married, Austin got an impressive letter in the mail from the Governor General of Canada, telling him that he had been chosen to be invested into the Order of Canada. Austin was incredibly excited, but crestfallen that I didn't seem to be. As an American, I really didn't understand how Canadian politics worked, let alone the British based honors system. To me, a governor is just the head of a state's government. The ones I have met in my life have been a seriously unimpressive lot. He very patiently explained that the Governor General was the head of Canada's government, the Queen's representative. I tried very hard to look very excited. I have hated formal functions my entire life, and I had a feeling this was going to be a doozy.

He had been nominated years before, originally, after he returned from the South Pole. Out of the blue, they had requested a wedding photo. I suspect they wanted to make sure that Austin was stable enough to endure the stress of receiving the award. I suppose if he was stable enough to get married, that meant he was stable enough to receive the award. Although, I sometimes joke that they wanted to make sure I wasn't a figment of his imagination. I might not have known at the time how important this award would eventually be for Austin, but I was happy at how excited he was. Not everyone was though. Surprisingly, his family was horrified. I was to learn that every time Austin received an award, this is how his family reacted. They were embarrassed that the family name made it into the paper linked with the word schizophrenia. He was getting screamed at on the phone.

He was being recognized by the government for two decades of advocacy for those with mental illnesses. When he became sick, his academic career came to an end. Even if he could have found a university willing to employ a schizophrenic, the politics of university life would have eaten him alive. He knew he needed a reason to get out of bed in the morning, so he began to volunteer. Over the years he gave hundreds of speeches, wrote numerous articles about mental illness for the newspaper, and advocated for programs in the community. He began to do university lectures both to undergraduate classes and in medical schools. Eventually he was named an adjunct professor at the University of Alberta. The Order of Canada recognizes those who give a life time of service to make Canada a better place. It is the highest civilian honor given in Canada.

As strange as his family's reaction seemed to me, something really interesting happened on my side. My mother, out of the blue, warmed up to Austin. She had always been a closet Anglophile. She was descended distantly from English royalty. She got up in the middle of the night to watch the wedding between Princess Diana and Prince Charles, as she did many years later for their son, Prince William's wedding. She decided if Austin was being decorated by the Queen's representative, it meant he must be okay. From then, they developed a close relationship; he spent more time on the phone with her than I did and sent her post cards almost every day. She admitted that she really couldn't read them, but she liked getting mail. Austin rarely had anything earth shattering to say in his cards, but loved writing them. It was a really weird relationship, but then everything involved with Austin has always been a bit weird.

The day of the ceremony, all the awardees looked terrified. Austin was convinced he was going to throw up or trip on national television. He was afraid that he would trip and fall on Michaëlle Jean, the Governor General at the time, and the RCMP would jump out and taser him. She is a petite woman who barely came up to Austin's shoulders even in heels. Later, he found out that everyone that day was afraid of throwing up or tripping. Austin was the only one afraid of being tasered though. During the formal reception later, I sat over out of the way; I enjoy people-watching. As the Governor General made her rounds speaking to all the recipients and their guests, she was followed by two plain clothed security guards. They had little ear pieces in their ears, and very much looked like the Secret Service agents that follow the US President around.

They actually looked a bit bored. Everyone in Rideau Hall that day was there by invitation, either as a recipient, or as one of their three allotted guests. They weren't expecting suicide bombers, and many of the recipients were senior citizens in the first place, since the Order of Canada is awarded for a lifetime of service. Austin was one of the youngest recipients present. As Michaëlle Jean approached Austin, her guards seemed to wake up, become attentive, and actually became a bit rigid. One put his hand inside his suit coat. I'm not sure if he was resting his hand on his gun or taser, but I got a bit alarmed. Michaëlle Jean was obviously not afraid. She got very close to Austin, and even placed her hand on his arm while they talked. She wanted to talk to him about the stigma he must face. I was afraid he might reach out to touch her and get jumped on. She would have had a first-hand view of stigma right in her face. Thankfully, he didn't, and she continued to speak to a famous musician next. Her bodyguards relaxed back into a near stupor.

I got Austin out of the middle of the room, just in case. Being overtired or under too much stress is toxic for someone with his illness, that includes good stress. After the formal dinner that night, we went back to the hotel with the older crowd. The younger guests stayed half the night listening to a jazz trio and dancing. Austin collapsed into bed. He woke up the next morning and started throwing up. I'd like to say it was just the abundance of rich food and wine the night before, but I knew it was his illness. It was as if that part of him hated that he was having such a good time. At least his family quit calling to scream at him after we got home.

I suppose my trip to Ottawa taught me a lot about becoming a Canadian. The highest civilian honor in the US is given mostly to famous people. In his ceremony there were some famous people, but mostly they were anonymous outside their hometowns. We sat at dinner with a woman who had immigrated to Canada after being a survivor of the Hiroshima bombing. Another immigrant at our table was from India and she had been an advocate for immigrant women in abusive relationships. Another was a retired professor from a small agriculture college, who had developed a new strain of barley that thrived in the cold. I met a missionary who had gone by snow mobile into the northern communities in the 50's. It taught me that Canada is a place made of lots of people from lots of places, and they came here not only to have a better life, but also to make Canada better, and they have. It inspired me to try to do the same.

TAKING IN STRAYS

Living with someone with schizophrenia isn't easy; nothing in life really worthwhile is. We live in an "interesting" part of town. That's not unusual for the disabled or mentally ill. We normally live on low fixed incomes, or are minimally employed. That means we need to live where it is cheap, or where we have access to the medical and social services we require, often both. Our neighbors are new immigrants getting on their feet, young artistic types, older residents who stayed when their neighborhoods went downhill, and those stuck in a cycle of poverty; usually due to drugs or alcohol. I've lived in similar neighborhoods in the United States. I suppose the main difference is the lack of firearms. The thugs in our neighborhood here are too poor to afford guns so they tend to stab each other. In any case, as long as you aren't wandering around at 3am looking for drugs or a prostitute, it's as safe as anywhere else.

I love it because it is so vibrant. We can eat the cuisine of a different country every day of the month without repeating. There are lots of young families and artists who live here for the low cost and atmosphere. Still, there are also lots of people who have been left behind by society or lost their way. Our first Christmas, I think because Austin was afraid I'd be lonely so far from my family, and he asked if I wanted to have a Christmas party. I'd always loved the ones my mom had, so I said yes. We were swarmed with people. It's not unusual for those with mental illnesses to be alienated from their friends and families. I think for a lot of them, just being invited to a party, even if they were too afraid to come, made them feel wanted.

We started having lots of parties. After Christmas there was Mardi Gras, then Easter, then birthdays, and Thanksgiving, both Canadian and American. It seemed like we were having one a month. One of the neighbors that often came with members of her family went to our church. She was the mother of nine, mostly adult children. She had a couple under 18 at home, and was also taking care of a couple of grandchildren. She had obviously lived a hard life. Her youngest son, Zach, was 11 when I met him. He was homeschooled and often came with his mother to daily mass. We decided the next winter to offer him $20 to shovel snow off the sidewalk in front of our condo. Later that afternoon, we saw a young man shoveling that we didn't know. Zach had paid him $5 to do the shoveling, pocketed the rest, and spent the afternoon playing video games. I was impressed. Apparently outsourcing had come to our little neighborhood.

Zach spent a lot of time at our apartment. He had lots of free time, and we always had little chores for him to do to earn pocket money. This kind of neighborhood was often short in one thing, and that were good male role models. Austin wasn't exactly the Marlboro Man, but he wasn't a drunk or drug addict, and most importantly, he was simply here. We helped his mother out whenever we could, which mostly meant driving her to the food bank after we finally got a car. She was collecting for 8-9 people and couldn't carry that much home without help. One night we got a call from her in the middle of the night. Zach had gotten arrested, and she needed our help/support to get him out. It was a serious offence, but he was just 16, and Canada still believes in treating juvenile offenders differently than adults. That was certainly different than his 25 year old accomplices.

It took us almost 24 hours to get him released on bail. Although this was his first offence, his police record contained several hits. At some time in the past, when his adult older brothers had been arrested, they had pretended to be Zach to get out as minors. He had to be finger printed so they could compare them to the ones taken when his brothers had been arrested. They finally got things straightened out, but he was placed in general population longer than a minor should have been. It was scary, and I suppose that was a good thing for him at the time. We decided at that point to try to take a more active interest in his welfare since Austin had vouched for him to get him released on his own recognizance.

The first thing we did was enroll him in the Army Cadets. Here they are rather a cross between Boy Scouts and Junior ROTC in the US. One thing he desperately needed was a place to find some better friends. For the first time in his life, he seemed to have found something to be proud of. We drove him to every meeting and campout. Sometimes that meant sitting in his driveway honking for an hour on a Saturday morning. We made sure he made it to court appearances, probation officer appointments, and kept his curfew. About a month after his arrest, when taking his mom to the food bank, I noticed something about her. She was quite out of breath after carrying just a couple of sacks out to the van. She was having crushing pain in her throat and shoulders. I knew that those were all symptoms of heart issues in women. I tried to urge her to go to her doctor. She said that she had already been, and it was diagnosed as gastric reflux and was told to treat it with bananas.

I knew his mom had been diagnosed with bipolar, but was one of those individuals who didn't believe in psychiatric medications. Austin had tried several times to get her to take one of Zach's older brothers, who had been having psychotic symptoms, to a doctor. She had originally taken Zach out of school in the first grade when they wanted to have him tested for ADHD. Having dealt with Arlene's illness for so long, I was well familiar with how distorted the thinking of someone with bipolar disorder can become when they aren't properly medicated. I had a long discussion with Austin about what we would do if something happened to Zach's mom.

We had discussed over a year before about the idea of adopting a child who had aged out of foster care without being adopted. We weren't going to have children of our own, but still felt the natural desire to have children. We were a bit old to think of adopting an infant. We had thought about becoming foster parents when we were still in the house, but didn't have that kind of room in our small condo. I was initially surprised they were okay with the idea that Austin had schizophrenia. The only thing they were interested in was making sure we had been a couple for at least a year, and had never been convicted of child abuse. We had signed up with the Boys and Girls Club as mentors for their program for emancipated minors and aged out foster children. We went to a lot of functions with the kids, but never really made a connection. When we had a discussion about Zach's mom, we both came to the agreement that if something happened to her, we would offer Zach a home.

Three months after he was arrested, I was expecting him and his mother for my Christmas Eve party. They didn't come. About 9pm, just as most of the last guests were leaving and I was in the kitchen beginning the clean-up, Zach appeared. He was crying so hard that he could barely speak. His mother was in the hospital. She'd had a heart attack right in front of him. By the time she made it to the hospital, her heart had been severely damaged. She lingered for a couple of days, and then passed away. Zach was inconsolable. He had spent almost 24 hours a day with his mom since 1st grade; she was his entire world. He was left in a home with two adult sisters and several nieces and nephews, and little money.

Thus began an odyssey that we never expected, really. First we rented an apartment for him upstairs from us. A few months after that, a unit came up for sale in our building. It was strange because the owner had told us repeatedly that he would never sell. Every condo has that one owner that makes things hard on everyone else. This guy had major depression and a major jerk streak. He kept a derelict van in his assigned space so he used a visitor space for his working vehicle. One summer he actually rented the van out to a homeless man to live in. He was a couple of years behind in condo fees, but had a paid off mortgage, so all we could threaten him with was a law suit. He didn't pay his court ordered child support, so I doubted taking him to court would have been worth the legal fees. He took over our upstairs storage room, changed the lock, and rented it out to a friend from work.

So when he told us that the city was going to sell his unit for back property taxes, we jumped on it. He left it in a state that I can't properly describe.

He had voodoo dolls hanging from hooks in the ceiling. There was blood on the walls in the master bedroom. He had an enormous collection of satanic books. Our funniest story from this horrific cleanup was our basset hound, Gandy, rooting through the piles of books, pulling out a satanic ritual book, and proceeding to tear it apart. He ripped the cover off, then promptly pooped on it, then sat barking at it. The picture was so hilarious that our priest put it on his Facebook for weeks. The bathroom had an enormous 4 foot wide hole to the studs in the shower. I guess we were lucky he didn't take many showers, since we were right below him.

There were too many repairs for me to make by myself, and Zach suggested one of his older brothers who was a contractor. So we started buying building materials, and his brother moved into the apartment. It was a nightmare. This brother was so much older than Zach that he never knew him growing up. All he knew was him coming to visit with a large expensive truck, telling everyone about his building jobs. He seemed to really need to have someone to look up to, and so he chose this one brother. It turns out that he was actually a drug dealer who knew little about construction. He and his friends once had a loud 3am painting party. Our neighbors were absolutely thrilled. I took over doing as much as I could. I had to buy all the paint and trim twice because he messed stuff up so badly the first time. Eventually, we got it habitable. His brother moved on, and is in jail as I'm writing this.

Thus began about two years of "adjustment." We were dealing with a young man who had come from such a dysfunctional family, that Dr. Phil could have filled an entire season with their stories. Zach was also dealing with severe grief and substance abuse issues. We were able to figure out really quickly that he had inherited his mother's mental illness as well. We got him into school and into counseling; neither went well. All the school did was allow him to hang out with other kids who were doing drugs, and the counseling kept ripping off the thin scabs he had grown over his wounds. We got him on some medication, and that seemed to help. We transferred him to a new school with smaller classes, designed for kids who have had interruptions in their schooling.

It was as if he was in the second grade in his ability to handle school. He's never had to sit still before, and he'd never had to meet a deadline for turning in an assignment. We quickly discovered the homeschool program his mom had used wasn't accredited with anyone. He had only really studied math and religion. To graduate he would need about 150 credits. After an entire year in school, he had been awarded a total of 5. By this time he was nearly 18 years old, and had a choice of going to school for at least 4 more years or getting a job. So, he got a job. It was just unloading donations to a thrift store, but he could do the work. He got a nice girlfriend from work and seemed to stabilize for a time.

Eventually he lost his job when he didn't show up on time. He started acting out again. We discovered that his girlfriend had gotten him off his medication. She belonged to a religion that didn't believe in psychiatrists. Knowing that he could get violent off his medication, she still seemed surprised when it happened, and dropped him quickly. After that, he had a parade of friends from school and the streets coming through his apartment. One was hiding from a step father who wanted to kill him, and another had been thrown out of his parent's house. He lived there for a couple of weeks and threatened to kill Zach if we kicked him out. We did anyway. He had a young couple from school move in who had serious alcohol issues. While drunk, this very small teenager liked to punch the walls. It cost us a couple of thousand dollars to replace all the doors, door jams and repair and repaint the damaged walls.

He had a roommate for a year that seemed to keep things calm at least, and then we found out that was because he was smoking pot to stupor every day. There was the friend who had such serious epilepsy that he couldn't hold a job for long. His mom had disappeared when he was little and his father was a crack addict. He got despondent and attempted suicide with his seizure medication. When he woke up from a coma weeks later, his father came to see him. He handed his son a steak knife and told him to use it next time he wanted to commit suicide so he could do it right. There was the boy who stole a car, but told Zach it was his, and they went for a ride. The car broke down and we went to get them. We

had a standing rule that anytime he needed us, he could call with no reper-
cussions. The night he got arrested, he didn't have a way home, and so
stayed and went along with the crowd. I didn't want that to happen again.

There are various other friends we tried to help. Another friend had a
severe case of fetal alcohol syndrome and was born addicted to cocaine.
He was living with his addict mother, her boyfriend and two younger
sisters when the boyfriend assaulted his sisters. Not wanting to lose her
boyfriend's paycheck, she placed the blame on her son. The police didn't
believe her, but took the boy out anyway, and he spent several years in
a secure home for juveniles who can't safely be placed in foster care.
While there he suffered an assault that caused him to lose a testicle
and was also covered in some kind of bites. There was another young
man who had lost his job and the only place he could afford to rent was
a room in a drug house. That's an extremely difficult place to live in if
you aren't doing drugs. He was kept up half the night by partiers, which
made it hard to get up in time to go to work. While at work, his room was
repeatedly broken into and robbed. The home had little heat or hot
water and so much mold that the carpet in his room was covered in
mushrooms. He had stapled a blanket down over it so he didn't have to
walk on them. After we got him out of there, he spent a week taking hot
showers and coughing up black goo.

It took a lot of patience. We both had to increase our blood pressure medicine. I knew that we weren't going to be successful with everyone that
came through our home. As a baseball fan, I know that it is the only sport
where you can fail 70% of the time and still be an all-star. Our hope was
that even those we had to kick out would receive some benefit from their
time with us. I hoped that sometime in the future, they would remember
something we had done or said and learn from it. I bought several pairs
of steel toed boots, hard hats and safety vests. All I asked of them is that
sometime in the future when they were our age, that they help a young
person get what they need in order to start a new job. Austin got their
paperwork in order. None of them ever seemed to have picture ID. We
got them into doctors and dentists. He filled out applications for them to

reclaim their lost First Nations status. He got them in for testing or counseling. He spent hours on the phones talking to bureaucrats and social workers.

All of these kids came into our lives through Zach. They were his friends or friends of friends. He has a very soft heart, and hated having a clean safe home and a full belly while his friends didn't. Unfortunately, he was too trusting. We should have realized that after the fiasco of hiring his brother. The most memorable evening was when he had one of those accidental social media parties. He had sent a friend on Facebook a message that he should come over to play a new video game. That friend posted it, and there ended up being more kids in there than the cops could count. There was a drunken naked teenage girl running across the front lawn. There was a fight downstairs that led to a broken glass security door. There were people jumping off the third floor balcony to avoid the police. The cops opened his bedroom closet to find it full of kids. They filed out like clowns from a mini car.

It was just so over the top that all we could do later was laugh about it and be thankful no one filmed it for YouTube. Downstairs, Zach was sitting on the floor against the wall watching his friends march out. One of the police constables asked Zach how old he was. He said 17. The cop said if he was his son, when he turned 18, he'd be out on the street. Zach looked instantly sober and looked up at me in terror. I crouched down next to him and told him that I didn't like the way he was acting, but I loved him unconditionally. That meant no matter what he did, I would not stop loving him. That if he committed murder, I would hate what he had done, but still love him. I would expect him to face the con-sequences of his actions, but I would be there every visiting day.

I told him that we were willing to adopt him if he felt that he wanted that kind of security. I told him that I would be proud to call him my son, but that I wasn't interested in replacing his mom. I described life like a pro wrestling match, something he could visualize. His mom got tired, and she needed to tag out; all we've done is tagged in. She did the hard part, and we would take it the rest of the way. We had the door fixed, cleaned up the mess, and banned certain people from the building. We ended up banning a lot of people eventually. He finally found a girlfriend who wanted him to stay on his medicine and stay clean and sober.

He was recognized with a major award from the Cadets. He was to be given it at the closing ceremonies of the year on a Sunday afternoon by the Lieutenant Governor who was a retired Colonel. He was really looking forward to it. Unfortunately, the ceremony fell on Father's Day. The day before, his family invited him to come to a party. They kept him there, giving him drugs and alcohol, knowing that they were preventing him from making it to his award ceremony. He was so sick, that when he finally came home on Sunday night, we almost took him to the hospital. They couldn't stand the idea of him getting an award, so they sabotaged it. He loved the Cadets, but it was really hard for him. Most kids start at the age of 12, so the kids in his unit were much younger than him. Kids his age were already sergeants or warrant officers. It didn't help that he was very tall. When he came to live with us, he was just over six feet tall. He grew six inches in the first two years. The running joke was that he never had to shine his cadet shoes. Every time they needed to be shined, he needed a bigger size so they just gave him bigger ones that came pre-shined. Eventually his feet got so large that they didn't make cadet shoes big enough, so they had to order regular army shoes for him.

After some time, as I spent lots more time with him, I began to realize that something was wrong. He loved Cadets, but had weeks that he just wouldn't go. I finally realized those were nights that they were going to have a test or lots of classroom work. If school was hard for him because he couldn't keep up with kids his own age, not being able to keep up with kids who were only 12 years old was devastating to his self-esteem. One of the things about growing up in a dysfunctional home is that kids become really good actors. They learn to act a certain way so that they don't get attacked or noticed. They become experts on mimicking normalcy. Over time, I recognized he had some deficits that were hard to get a handle on. As an example, I realized that he only had three words to explain emotions he was feeling; happy, mad or sad. The special school downtown had promised to test Zach to see where he was academically and what type of remedial help he needed. It turns out they really had no desire to help him. Their only interest was in filling out the forms for his diagnosis of bipolar so that the province would give them significantly more money to have him enrolled. They didn't care if he attended school. They didn't care if he did any work. So long as they had him on their books, they could claim lots of special education funding for him.

Austin had a contact at the local rehabilitation hospital that does some involved testing for adults who are suspected of having fetal alcohol syndrome. We knew that his mother had drunk alcohol heavily until Zach was 4 years old. He thought that the fetal alcohol issue was kind of a minor one, but would get him in the door to get some needed testing. We knew he had been diagnosed with bipolar disorder and PTSD. He had also had several really serious head injuries from the violence present in his home. The testing lasted three days. At the end, he was exhausted and silent. Finally, he just looked up and said, "I really have it, don't I?" He had never experienced getting sent to the principal. He had never repeated a grade. He had never really tried to sit still in a class room for a long term. He had never had any kind of school testing. The things that he might have experienced attending a regular school that might have prepared him to understand that he wasn't like other kids, he had never experienced. Taking the testing, and the difficulty he had with it, brought him 18 years' worth of insight and understanding all at once.

We had been prepared to hear some pretty harsh realities when we went into the clinic to hear the results of his testing. When we saw a dozen people in the room, we were really scared. There were social workers, psychiatric nurses, neurology technicians, and even a couple of trainees. He certainly wasn't the worst subject that came through, but he had profound deficits, much more than we could possibly have guessed. The saving grace was that the results of the testing were over his head, so it didn't make him feel bad about himself, just tired. When we originally took him in, I suppose we had it in mind that we could get him some training, maybe a tradesman ticket, and launch him into adulthood. After that day, we realized that we were now responsible for a young man who was permanently disabled, and would always need support. In a way though, we probably were gifted with a child whose hurdles in life might well be on par with that of any natural child we might have had together and would have been born with.

We decided to wait until Zach was 18 to adopt him for several reasons. We had already re-written our wills so that he was our only heir, so it wasn't a necessary financial step. We were trying to be mindful of members of his family who were very angry at us for taking him in. Some were unhappy because we weren't family. There were over 200 people at his mother's funeral, but we were the only ones who asked him if he had a place to go. Some were angry that he was being taken care of when they weren't. One of his uncles was very angry that we had applied for him to go on disability, calling those on assistance as parasites. We did it primarily to make sure he could continue to receive his medication. It was also a way to provide a basic level of support for him since he would probably never be able to hold more than a part time job.

One of his older sisters developed a seizure disorder, in part due to a con-genital defect in the veins in her brain and partly because of the extreme amount of drug use she was engaging in. She once collapsed in the parking lot of the grocery store next door. When the EMT's arrived, she didn't have a pulse, but they were able to bring her back. Zach rode his bike by just in time to see her being worked on. When the social workers at the hospital attempted to sign her up for disability so that she could get into a long term treatment facility, her family became furious. They all told her that she shouldn't go on disability; they told her to just raise dogs to make money, or make money off her "habits". That was their code word for becoming a drug dealer or prostitute I suppose. Zach's family was so dysfunctional that it was deemed to be far better to become a drug dealer than to accept public assistance to get clean and sober.

Another reason we wanted to wait until he was 18 to adopt him is that we wouldn't have to fight with his family for permission. When we originally took him in, we needed to find his father in order to get a guardianship form signed so that we would be able to get him into the doctor. He was living in a homeless shelter downtown. He was very willing to sign, but thought it was weird. At 17, he expected Zach to just be out on his own supporting himself. All we had to do then was buy him lunch to get him to sign; we didn't want to have to go through that again. Plus, his dad was the kind that didn't mind if someone else had to financially support his kids, but if that child no longer wanted his last name, that would have caused all sorts of "ownership" issues.

We faced a lot of opposition, both officially and unofficially. Trying to get him on the health insurance was a nightmare. He had been on his mother's insurance card. So the minute that she died, he officially had no insurance in a province where everyone has insurance. We had to take it up to the Minister of Health to get that sorted out. The social workers investigated us; we had two of them sit in our parking lot taking pictures of our coming and going. The idea that someone would adopt a troubled teenager in our neighborhood was beyond understanding. If we had adopted a child from Africa or Central America, no one would have batted an eye. Adopting an orphan in our own neighborhood was such a strange idea that we must have had some kind of ulterior motive.

To me, it felt like marrying Austin all over again. People thought we must be up to something. I'm still not sure if they thought we were tricking him out for sexual favors or we were using him to run drugs for us. Social workers and teachers, members of his family, and more friends that I would have thought possible, all believed we were either up to something or being played for chumps. There were a few close friends who really understood. They were afraid for us, but supported us. I'm not sure we could have endured it but for those few with us. It was very hard at times, but with most things in life, the things that are hardest are also usually the most rewarding. When Zach had PTSD flashbacks, I could help him through them because I have them too. When his bipolar symptoms flared up, I knew what to do because I'd dealt with every single one of them during the years I lived with Arlene.

When I married Austin, I told him that all I expected from him was to live as happy and as healthy a life as he was capable of. That now extended to Zach. One day while we were driving in the car, he told me that he thought he'd be dead if we hadn't taken him in. I told him that Austin and I both almost died when we weren't much older than he was now. God saved us for a reason. He gave each of us hurdles and experiences in life that made us ideally situated and capable of taking care of him. I told him that God may have saved him to do something that he can't possibly conceive right now. When it comes, he just has to be ready to accept the challenge. Considering the path he was headed down, we might have saved more than his life. We might have saved the life of someone Zach might have killed. The doctors at the rehabilitation hospital told us that he was either headed to jail or the morgue when we took him in.

In the sweep of a judge's pen, Zach became our son, and the only kid in the neighborhood who had a mother and father who were still married and weren't alcoholics or addicts. We realized that acutely one day when he walked in on us having an argument. Austin and I don't fight very often, but like every normal couple, we do fight. Although I'm told I'm infuriating to have a fight with because all my mediation training makes it like trying to step on the same drop of water in a stream twice. We apologized to him for having to see us fight. He started to laugh so hard that I thought he was going to wet himself. He informed us that if there wasn't blood or things being broken, it wasn't a real fight. He had never learned what being in a real classroom was like. It was the same for never having seen how real men and women can have a dispute and fight fairly. It reminded us that we had to not only teach by our words, but also by our actions.

CONCLUSION

The story isn't over yet. I'm sure my travels among the eccentric and disenfranchised will continue. I've known so many interesting people in my life, and each one taught me something. My Dad was right about God giving us challenges in order to strengthen the spiritual muscles we will need later. The two hardest were certainly David and Arlene. Without them I would never have known how to help Zach. Their lives were both too short, but valuable. I miss them both. I'd like to think that freed from their very human bodies, they are free from pain and heartache. I hope they forgive me for the mistakes I made with them both, just as I hope Austin and Zach forgive the mistakes I still make. As I constantly remind them, and myself, progress not perfection.